The
Physical Basis
of
Mental Illness

The Physical Basis
of
Mental Illness

Ronald Chase

Transaction Publishers
New Brunswick (U.S.A.) and London (U.K.)

The cover illustration, titled "Scared and Hiding," is by Rodger Casier. It was provided by NARSAD Artworks, which promotes the creative work of persons with mental illness. Proceeds go to the Brain & Behavior Research Foundation (formerly NARSAD).

This book is printed on acid-free paper that meets the American National Standard for Permanence of Paper for Printed Library Materials.

Library of Congress Catalog Number: 2011009016
ISBN: 978-1-4128-4264-8
Printed in the United States of America

Library of Congress Cataloging-in-Publication Data

Chase, Ronald.
    The physical basis of mental illness / Ronald Chase.
        p. ; cm.
    Includes bibliographical references.
    ISBN 978-1-4128-4264-8 (alk. paper)
    1. Mental illness--Physiological aspects.   2. Psychophysiology.
I. Title.
    [DNLM: 1. Mental Disorders—psychology.   2. Mental Disorders—physiopathology.   3. Mental Processes—physiology.   4. Philosophy, Medical. 5.   Psychoanalytic Theory.
  6.   Psychophysiology. WM 140]
    RC455.4.B5.C47 2011
    616.89—dc22
                                                    2011009016

For Dorothy

Contents

Preface

This book is intended not only for academics and psychiatric professionals, but also for anyone who has been affected by mental illness—victims, family members, and caregivers. Mental illness arouses an intense curiosity, and people are challenged to reconcile conflicting interpretations. Regrettably, they get little help from the popular media. While stories about the brain and the mind appear frequently on television, in the printed media, and on the Web, the coverage is superficial and inadequate. I hope that my account will go some way toward correcting this deficiency. I have endeavored to present a conception of mental illness that is consistent with current developments in both the philosophy of mind and the science of psychopathology.

Humans tend to imagine *stuff* when they are faced with things that they do not understand. In ancient times, people watched with keen interest the movements of the stars and planets, but they were perplexed, unable to account for the changing sky. Then Aristotle, together with others, came up with the idea of the aether. It was supposed to be an invisible, unchanging substance that filled the sky. The aether was called the fifth natural element, the quintessence, after air, water, fire, and earth. An important property of the aether was that it moved constantly in circles. Thus, because the celestial bodies were thought to be embedded in the aether, their movements were explained, or so it seemed. Much later, Isaac Newton showed that this explanation could not possibly be true. By that time, however, other uses for the aether had been invented, principally it was said to be the substance that carries light through space. In 1887, two physicists, Albert Michelson and Edward Morley, set out to measure the aether. Despite their use of highly sensitive techniques, they were not able to detect any aether at all. Still, it was not until 1905 that Albert Einstein's special theory of relativity (1905) delivered the death blow; today, only a few die-hard enthusiasts believe in the aether.

The supposition that humans possess a mind completely separate from anything material is another idea with a long history but a dubious future. Nearly 500 years ago, the French philosopher and essayist René Descartes wrote that the mind, or soul, is an actual *thing* that exists independently of the body and that interacts with the brain. It is the mind, not the brain, which thinks, feels, and experiences life. Descartes' philosophy, called dualism, has survived to the present day because it has a strong intuitive appeal. However, intuitions can give a false sense of reality. When it comes to mental illness, the philosophy of dualism leads one to assume that mental illness is, literally, *in the mind.* I believe that Descartes' conception of the mind is misconceived and, therefore, the term mental illness is misleading and confusing. Moreover, stigma and other harmful consequences follow from the idea that there can be illnesses *in the mind.* Mental illness is a brain disease, not an illness of the mind.

Philosophy and science share the common goal of understanding the world in which we live. Philosophers need to keep apprised of new scientific discoveries so that their ideas remain relevant, and scientists need philosophy to help them put their work in perspective. Hence, each enterprise feeds off the other, and the leading edges of the two disciplines tend to converge on a common understanding of basic issues. Descartes' philosophy, for example, combined a fascination with mechanics, popular in the seventeenth century, with a deep religious faith, also common at the time. Presently, in the early years of the twenty-first century, we are experiencing another such convergence of science and philosophy, one that is likely to have significant consequences for society, not unlike those that occurred during the European Renaissance. A new world view is emerging based on materialistic philosophies and the knowledge brought forth by scientific enquiry.

Nature magazine, the leading international journal of science, recently highlighted the changes taking place in psychiatry by proclaiming, "There are many ways in which the understanding and treatment of conditions such as schizophrenia are ripe for a revolution." In the opinion piece that appeared beneath the foregoing title, the editors wrote, "The stigma of psychiatric disorders is misplaced, their burdens of society are significantly greater than more publicized diseases in developed and developing nationals alike, and biomedical science is poised to make significant strides."[1]

Thomas R. Insel, director the National Institute of Mental Health (USA), confirms the shifting intellectual ground in the following personal testimony.

> Much of what I learned as a resident in psychiatry 30 years ago has been proven utterly wrong. At that time, we believed that peptic ulcer disease was due to intrapsychic conflicts treatable with psychoanalysis; autism resulted from rigid, cold mothers who drove their children into psychic isolation; and schizophrenia could be treated through a regressive process allowing the patient to "work through" the psychosis as a growth experience. Now, these and other myths have been discarded as a result of scientific research.[2]

This book celebrates the new biological psychiatry while advancing a rational approach to the phenomenon of mental illness that keeps pace with the science. The sooner medical professionals, caregivers, and the general population adopt views that are realistic and philosophically sound, the better will psychiatric patients fare.

The book begins with three vignettes about ordinary people trying to come to terms with mental illness. Hopefully, these fictional pieces will ground the following discussion, which may otherwise suffer the remoteness of scholarship. To portray a range of attitudes and responses, I have chosen to depict events at three different times in history. The first two vignettes are entirely imaginary, while the third is drawn from my personal experience.

I thank Dorothy Chase for advice and encouragement.

Notes

1.   Nature, 2010.
2.   Insel, 2009.

1

Three Historical Vignettes

Athens, 470 BC

Three young men are walking down the road from Athens to the *Academia*.[1] Menexenus, the son of Socrates, is a student at the *Academia*, and he is eagerly anticipating another day of thoughtful discourse with his teacher, Plato. Jason and Niko are friends of Menexenus; they have come along because they want to harvest olives in the groves surrounding the *Academia*. After having walked about a half mile from the Dipylon Gates of Athens, all three men suddenly turn their eyes to observe a bony, bearded man crouching naked among the gravestones at the side of the road. At first glance, it appears that he is bending an arrow toward a target in the trees, but then the travelers note that the old man is holding nothing in his hands. "The furies! The furies!" he shouts, as he thrashes about and points his imaginary arrow first here, then there. He is wild-eyed, filthy, and foaming at the mouth. The three friends immediately realize that the old man is mad, so they approach him to learn more. "Dionysus told me to slaughter my mother and remove her eyes, and I have done so," says the old man. "Everywhere now, these furies pursue me to avenge my mother's death. It is because of this that I neither eat nor drink. I fear being poisoned, and I go sleepless lest the furies strike me in bed. Even here, where lies the remains of my mother, the furies torment me, and so I shoot my arrows."

"Clearly," says Niko, "this man is being punished for murdering his mother. Perhaps he is also the victim of a family curse. Whatever is at the root of it, the god Dionysus has now entered into his being so that he and Dionysus are like one. Together, they are pursued by the furies whose special interest, as you know, is avenging the wrongs done to parents and ancestors. Only Apollo or another powerful god can bring relief, but I do not expect that they will do that."

Without directly contradicting anything said by Niko, Jason suggests a practical course of action. "We could help the man," he says, "by

1

bringing him to a follower of Hippocrates. This wise man has taught us that thoughts and actions come from the brain, while intelligence and feelings come from the air, through breathing. The mad man's brain has become dry and cold, and that is why he behaves the way he does. No doubt the liver has released a great amount of black bile, which has produced these changes in the brain. We could help this unfortunate man by giving him white hellebore to eat. Hippocrates gave hellebore to his friend Democritus when he too was mad, and it seemed to help. The bitterness of this herb makes one vomit, but it also relieves madness."

The mad man grabs hold of a young olive tree and shakes it violently as if to dislodge spirits hiding in its canopy. Meanwhile, Menexenus, who has so far remained silent, can no longer hold his tongue. "My dear friends," says Menexenus, "I don't disagree with anything that you have said, but your accounts of this man's difficulties make no mention of his soul. Can't you see that his soul is in turmoil? It is the sickness of his soul that is responsible for these actions that we behold. By sickness I mean, of course, that the three parts of the soul—reason, passion, and appetite—have become disordered. Justice and good health dictate that reason must rule because reason is divine and immortal, whereas the irrational elements of the soul are merely material. When appetite gains control, people act in bizarre ways. It is the same with the soul as it is with our political state: all parts must work in perfect harmony. You should read Plato's dialogues, *The Republic* and *Phaedrus*, to learn how to maintain harmony within the soul, for in this way you can prevent madness."

Strasbourg, AD 1585

Manfred, troubled by his sister's behavior, takes her to see the parish priest, Father Johannes.[2] The priest's home is cold and dark, lit only by a fire burning in the hearth. "My dear Marta," says Father Johannes, "why do you wail with discontent? I remember you as a sweet child chasing butterflies in the fields, but now your brother tells me that you refuse to leave your house and that you act strangely. You shout out peoples' names, and you knock your head against the wall until blood flows down your cheeks. What is the matter?" Marta wipes away some tears and begins to tell her story.

"It started one day in early summer when Aunt Freda told me that I must go upstairs. As soon as I entered the bedroom, I saw fifteen men wearing the knights' green clothing. Fifteen men! She said that I must choose one of these men to take as my husband. At first I refused, and I was beaten until I bled. When I could no longer resist, I pointed to the smallest of the men. I lost my flower in the hours that followed. After that, Aunt Freda often transported me, at night, over vast distances. One night she took me from Strasbourg to Cologne."

Although feigning surprise at Marta's tale, Father Johannes antici- pates something of the sort, for he is aware that Marta's Aunt Freda has already been burned as a witch. Thus, he knows that Marta is pos- sessed by a devil. He knows, too, that only those who have forsaken the faith can succumb to a witch's inducements and become possessed. So Father Johannes is torn between sympathy and duty. He recognizes her pain, but he is also aware of his responsibility to keep the parish free of all types of evil, principally the evil inherent in devils, witches, sorcerers, succubae, incubi, and werewolves.

Father Johannes has additional troubling thoughts that he can- not share with anyone. Like his contemporary, the French essayist Montaigne, he questions the powers attributed to witches. How is it possible, for example, that a witch can transport Marta overnight from Strasbourg to Cologne? No horse can gallop so fast. Also, how can he reconcile his readings that speak of excessive black bile as the cause of crazy behaviors with the church's position that black bile is simply the proximate cause of madness, while the devil is the ultimate cause. What, exactly, does all of this mean?

His thoughts turn to the text, *Antipalus Maleficiorum* (The Enemy of Witchcraft, 1508), from the pen of Johannes Trithemius. This other Johannes was a Benedictine abbot, greatly admired for his wisdom and gentleness. Father Johannes picks up the document and reads, "There is no part in our body that the witches would not injure. Most of the time they make human beings possessed and thus they are left to the devils to be tortured with unheard-of pains. They even get into carnal relations with them. Unfortunately, the number of such witches is very great in every province . . . . Yet Inquisitors and judges who could avenge these offenses against God and nature are few and far between . . . . Many suffer constantly from the most severe diseases and are not even aware that they are bewitched."

With all of this bubbling in his mind, Father Johannes faces a difficult, practical decision. Should he excuse Marta by administering a holy unction, or should he allow her to be prosecuted and punished? In the end, a passage recalled from Pope Innocent VIII's bull, *Summis desider- antes affectibus* (Desiring with Supreme Ardor, 1484) settles the matter.

In this declaration, the pope had proclaimed, "All heretical depravity should be driven far from the frontiers and bournes of the Faithful." And so, Father Johannes takes Marta to the local prosecutor.

Some weeks later, Marta is brought before the judge. Her body has been shaved from head to feet, so that no devil can conceal himself within the hair, and her nakedness reveals many marks of torture. As a further precaution, she is made to walk backward into the court so that she cannot bewitch the judge by gazing upon him with her evil eyes. Peter, the judge, is a no nonsense kind of guy. He obediently looks to the *Malleus Maleficarum* (the Witches' Hammer, ca. 1488) for inspiration, interpretation, and instruction. It is obvious to him that Marta is possessed by the devil. Furthermore, it matters not that she may have imagined certain events like the overnight transport from Strasbourg to Cologne, for this very possibility is dealt with in the *Malleus Maleficarum*, "The art of riding abroad may be merely illusory, since the devil has extraordinary power over the minds of those who have given themselves up to him, so that what they do in pure imagination, they believe they have actually and really done in the body." In other words, the devil produces not only the witch's evil acts, but also her deluded thoughts of evil acts. Finally, as also stated in the *Malleus Maleficarum*, anyone who succumbs to the devil's influence is guilty of having a weak will and has thereby sinned by voluntarily allowing the devil to take control over his or her soul. The only way to free the soul is to burn the body. Judge Peter agrees with all of this, so his decision comes quickly. He declares Marta a witch, and he condemns her to death by auto-da-fé.

Los Angeles, AD 1960

We are driving on the Golden State Freeway heading north toward Los Angeles city center, and beyond that, home. Or rather, my dad is driving; Mom is seated next to him, and I am in the backseat. The summer air is hot, dry, and smoggy. We are returning from a visit to the Metropolitan State Hospital, Norwalk, where my brother Jim is a patient. Jim is twenty-six years old, tall, thin, and schizophrenic; I am seven years younger. Two years ago, while studying for a graduate degree in English literature at UCLA, Jim phoned Mom to say that he had a gun and he intended to kill himself. Now, only a few weeks later, he has already been in three hospitals. Before he dies, he will know thirteen different hospitals and at least nine psychiatric residences. His symptoms include many of those that are typically associated with schizophrenia, namely paranoia, auditory hallucinations, depression, and anger. Jim and I have traveled together, played ping-pong, basketball, and chess, joked, and argued.

Two days ago, Jim was given electroconvulsive shock. Earlier, at the Edgemont Hospital in Hollywood, he was given insulin-induced shock. These are supposed to be therapies, and both procedures seemed to help, but only temporarily. Each time, his unpredictable, uncontrollable behavior returned after a few days.

Traveling home after the visit, the dismal atmosphere of the hospital still fills our car. We recall how the hospital staff had made us wait for more than an hour outside a heavily secured glass door before Jim was let out, and then we were obliged to speak with him inside a small public area that held only basic physical comforts. To make matters worse, Jim said little today. Not that he is very talkative at the best of times, but today he was both silent and sullen. Recalling all of this as we speed along the freeway, none of us is feeling optimistic.

I lean forward to ask my mother in the front seat, "How does electroconvulsive shock therapy work, anyway?"

She turns her head around to reply, "Dr. Held told me that it clears the mind."

"Clears the mind of what? And, what's left in the mind afterward? I don't understand this shock therapy."

"It's very complicated, Ron, and I'm only beginning to understand these things myself, thanks to Sigmund Freud. Freud is a rare genius, he and Albert Einstein. You've read some of Freud's books, so maybe you know that there are three parts to the mind: the ego, the id, and the superego. The ego is essentially our conscious self. It makes decisions and dictates our actions. The id represents our basic biological needs like hunger and sex. These instincts exert powerful, but unconscious, influences on the ego. The superego is also an unconscious part of the mind. It acts like a counterweight to the id because it represents religious and moral values. Do you know about psychodynamic conflict? The id may urge the ego to do one thing, while the superego tells it not do that very same thing. These conflicts can take over the mind and cause schizophrenia. This is why Jim has been seeing Dr. Held for the past several years, to uncover his unconscious conflicts. Anyway, whatever is the nature of his conflicts, the electrical shocks are supposed to get rid of them. Once that happens, he'll be free of those pent up energies that make him so withdrawn and irritable."

After a pause, my mother continues, "There is something else that is important for you to understand. You are mature enough so that I do not have to hide any of this from you. Conflicts also come from within the family—like in our family. You know how difficult it is sometimes at the dinner table. The tension, it can be unbearable."

"Mom, you do not have to tell me about tensions in the family!"

Dad keeps his eyes on the road. He does not join in the conversation. He has no interest in psychology.

Mom continues, "Sure, Ron, I know that you suffer from this situation as much any of us. Still, we should try to understand what Freud says. I'm sure you have heard of the Oedipus complex, where the boy loves his mother and is jealous of his father. Who knows, maybe Jim has this. And, let me tell you, I have heard that some analysts blame the mothers of schizophrenics for causing conflicts in their children. I don't buy it. In fact, I really do not know how any of this applies to us. I've always loved Jim, and I think he loves me. To tell you the truth, I trust Freud, but I just don't understand how sex explains Jim's condition. Maybe his sexual conflicts are buried too deeply for us to see them.

"Deep inside of what?" I said, "Where is the mind, anyway? And, what about the brain? Are they shocking Jim's brain or his mind? I mean, I just cannot figure how shocking the brain is going to resolve a conflict between the id and the superego. Nor for that matter do I understand what, exactly, *is* the id and the superego. The ego is more or less familiar, but since the other things are not part of our consciousness, how do we know that they actually exist? I really wish I knew how the brain works."

Dad is finally ready to state his position. "I don't know about any of this sex stuff or any supposedly unconscious conflicts. All I know is that Jim had some bad experiences over there at UCLA. He's an intelligent boy, and he'll get over it."

Notes

1. The portrayal of the mad man in the fourth-century BC Greek narrative is loosely based on the tragic plays *Orestes* and *Bacchae*, both by Euripides. The interpretations of bizarre behavior are based on Zilboorg, 1941, Simon, 1978, and Roccatagliata, 1986.

2. Marta's narrative from sixteenth-century Stausbourg is based on material found in Zilboorg, 1941, and Roccatagliata, 1986. The quotations from *Antipalus Maleficiorum, Summis desiderantes affectibus,* and *Malleus Maleficarum* are taken from Zilboorg, 1941.

2

The Search for Understanding

Mental illness is easy to recognize, but difficult to explain. When a family member spends hours at a time alone in his or her room mumbling incoherently to himself or herself or when our child is consistently indifferent to our loving attentions, we suspect that the person is mentally ill. Likewise, if a friend says that he is Jesus Christ and he will heal us of an ailment, or a neighbor cuts his lawn every day and meticulously removes every tiny bit of debris, in these cases, too, we think of mental illness. By contrast, we recognize mental health by rational behaviors, sociability, and the ability to enjoy life even while coping with its inevitable difficulties.

We call these conditions mental illness, but what do we actually mean by this label? And, why does it matter what we call it? The truth is that difficult philosophical and scientific problems lie beyond our casual familiarity with mental illness. Such problems inevitably attract the interest of academic scholars, but they also weigh heavily, I believe, on how we relate to, and deal with, mentally ill individuals. Whether our role is that of a family member, a psychiatric professional, or simply a fellow citizen, our approach to the disturbed person depends on our understanding of his or her condition. People tend to be uncertain about the causes of mental illness, unable to decide whether it is due to brain problems, psychological problems, weak wills, or fate. Often the victims themselves are at a loss to explain exactly what is wrong, and how things got to be as they are. Ignorance leads to inappropriate responses, which may include stigmatization with its attendant loss of friends, jobs, and respect. By contrast, someone who has a disease like diabetes, cancer, or Alzheimer's is understood to suffer from a problem of dysfunctional cells or organs. The victim of these diseases is treated with dignity and compassion. What is special about mental illness that brings these additional social burdens? I believe that one of the reasons why people mistreat the victims of mental illness, perhaps the main reason, is because they have confused or erroneous ideas about the condition, some of which are fundamentally philosophical.

The term *mental illness* first appeared, appropriately as we will see, in a work of fiction. Emily Brontë used it in her novel *Wuthering Heights*, published in 1847. Physicians may have adopted the term after reading Emily Brontë's novel, or from other influences. In either case, the medical profession quickly adopted the term, and it was already widely accepted by the end of the nineteenth century. Ms. Brontë was not a physician, so she most likely used the term as a metaphor to describe her character's state of mind. Plato (c. 427–347 BC) also used metaphors of illness, one of which, "scars of the soul," was mentioned in his dialogue *Gorgias*.[1]

Whatever the original intentions of Plato and Brontë, I believe that many people today, perhaps most people, understand the term mental illness in its literal, not metaphorical, sense. Crucially, therefore, we need to recognize the two key components of the term, literally understood. First, it states that the behaviors referred to constitute a medical condition, and second, it declares that the illness is *in the mind*, whereas all other illnesses are *in the body*. Thus, we are led to a critical examination of the separate concepts of illness and mind. We begin with the simpler task, the meaning of illness.

The Meaning of Illness

The exact definition of illness is somewhat controversial. One issue revolves around putative differences between *illnesses, diseases,* and *disorders*.[2] I, however, see no useful distinction between any of these terms, so I will use them interchangeably. Note also that I favor abandoning the term *mental illness*, and I will suggest alternatives at the end of this book. Nevertheless, in the absence of a consensus alternative, I am compelled, by convention and practical needs, to speak of mental illness throughout this book.

The philosopher of science, Rachel Cooper, discusses five competing "accounts" of the word.[3] According to one influential account, that of Christopher Boorse, a value-free definition is required. He says, quite simply, that a condition should be designated as an illness only when there is a dysfunction in some biological system.[4] Cooper, on the other hand, argues persuasively for a multifaceted definition in which the condition must be a harmful and medically treatable, and the person suffering from the condition must be seen as "unlucky." After a lengthy discussion, however, she concedes, "There is much work still to be done with developing an account of disease."[5]

Regardless of which formal definition of illness one wishes to adopt, it is clear that when people either hear or utter the words "mental illness," they infer that the person exhibiting bizarre or uncontrolled behavior is sick. The label evokes an interpretation based on the so-called medical model. The basic idea of the medical model dates to at least Hippocrates (460–377 BC), the acknowledged "father of medicine." While Hippocrates was mostly concerned with physical disorders, he also considered cases that we, today, characterize as mental illnesses. Hence, Hippocrates is usually credited with originating the medical model of mental illness. He thought that all diseases, whether manifested by physical aberrations or by mental aberrations, are caused by physical events and should be treated by physical means. Mental disorders, he thought, reflect abnormal brain conditions caused by the accumulation of toxins. The four toxins of special concern, called humors, are phlegm, yellow bile, black bile, and blood. The following text, which covers his understanding of mental illness, is extraordinary because it unambiguously identifies the brain as the organ responsible for both mentality and behavior, and it proposes specific biological causes for mental disturbances. Although generally attributed to Hippocrates, the text may, in fact, have been written by one of his students.

> Men ought to know that from nothing else but the brain come joys, delights, laughter and sports, and sorrows, griefs, despondency, and lamentations. And by this, in an especial manner, we acquire wisdom and knowledge, and see and hear, and know what are foul and what are fair, what are bad and what are good, what are sweet, and what unsavory . . . . And by the same organ we become mad and delirious, and fears and terrors assail us, some by night, and some by day, and dreams and untimely wanderings, and cares that are not suitable, and ignorance of present circumstances, desuetude, and unskilfulness [sic]. All these things we endure from the brain, when it is not healthy, but is more hot, more cold, more moist, or more dry than natural, or when it suffers any other preternatural and unusual affection . . . . As long as the brain is at rest, the man enjoys his reason, but the depravement of the brain arises from phlegm and bile, either of which you may recognize in this manner: Those who are mad from phlegm are quiet, and do not cry out nor make a noise; but those from bile are vociferous, malignant, and will not be quiet, but are always doing something improper.[6]

Hippocrates's medical model of mental illness includes two key components. First, it states that mental illness is indeed an illness. Second, it assumes that the illness resides in the body. This is the same type of explanation for mental illness to which I myself subscribe. Others, however, accept the medical model but think that the illness is in the mind. The difference between these views rests on differing concepts of the mind.

The Meaning of Mind

If the meaning of illness is mildly contentious, the meaning of mind is beset with unmatched controversy; it is one of the most perplexing problems in philosophy. Further, if any philosophical problem is to be called *metaphysical*, questions concerning the nature of mind would certainly qualify, although the precise meaning of metaphysical is itself uncertain. In any case, philosophers divide into two main camps regarding the status of mind. Some believe that the mind is a real thing and that it exists separately from the brain; this is the philosophy of *dualism.* The most influential of all dualist authors is Réne Descartes (1596–1650), whose works will be discussed in the next chapter. Briefly, dualists maintain that mind and its contents reside in an immaterial space. Furthermore, according to the most common variety of dualism, the mind can influence the brain and, by this means, it can cause behavior. Other philosophers say that the mind has no independent existence and that it is just a property or a product of the brain's physiological activity; this is the philosophy of *monism.* In this view, there are only physical things in the world, and that which we call mind only represents an aspect of one particular physical thing (the human brain) or maybe a class of physical things, the latter possibly including animal brains and computers.

The distinction between monism and dualism is crucial for understanding mental illness. The literal interpretation of mental illness as an illness *in the mind* is an interpretation based in dualism. It assumes that there *is* a mind separate from the brain. If, on the contrary, one assumes that mental phenomena are nothing but aspects of activity in the physical brain (monism), then there is only the brain to become ill. In the latter case, the term mental illness may be politically correct, but factually misleading. In my opinion, the monist philosophies (there are different versions, as I will describe) provide a more realistic account of mind and a better outlook on mental illness.

A dualistic mode of thought is responsible for the common, literal interpretation of the term mental illness, for only if there *is* a substantive mind can there be an illness *in* or *of* the mind. Despite some serious flaws in the philosophical arguments that claim to support dualism, dualism exerts a strong, albeit tacit, influence in most peoples' lives. I believe that this fact accounts for much of the miscomprehension of mental illness. Therefore, in the next chapter, I will examine dualism more closely by reviewing its origins, outlining its principles, and critiquing its arguments.

Many people think that the mind is a mysterious thing that cannot be understood. They do not even try to make sense of it. Others try, but they get lost in thinking about immaterial things that interact with material things. Even academic philosophers, whose job it is to think seriously about mind, argue vociferously about basic issues, and they too get discouraged. None of this, however, will deter us from tackling the key problems in the philosophy of mind as they affect mental illness. A little philosophy can go a long way in helping us to think clearly and correctly about mental illness.

Physical versus Psychological Versions of the Medical Model

As I stated above, Hippocrates's medical model for mental illness is grounded in the assumption that physiological abnormalities account for the condition. His specific hypothesis concerning the role of humors was credible as late as the 1800s, but obviously never proven. In fact, there was no indisputable evidence for any type of physical abnormality until late in the twentieth century.[7] In the intervening period, when physical evidence was lacking, an alternative version of the medical model for mental disturbances emerged, one which emphasizes the psychological dimension more than the physical dimension. The psychological version of the medical model is of particular interest because it is associated with dualism.

Important developments in the second half of the nineteenth century resulted in a major division of the medical model, and remnants of this split remain relevant today.[8] The developments of which I speak occurred at a time during which the patient population at insane asylums was increasing dramatically. Some historians attribute the growth to a real increase in the incidence of mental illness, while others attribute it to social and economic factors. Whatever the cause or causes, the highly profitable asylums generally and they generally delivered humane, but ineffective, treatments. They also offered incentives to scientists searching for the biological causes of mental illness.

A leading German psychiatrist, Emil Kraepelin (1856–1926), brought several prominent research anatomists to his clinic at Heidelberg. Among this group were several men who were to make important discoveries in brain science, such as Franz Nissl and Aloys Alzheimer. They faced a huge challenge, however, in their search for the microscopic signatures of mental illness. As time wore on with no breakthrough discoveries, Kraepelin turned his attention to other things, namely the vexing issue of diagnosis. Eventually, Kraepelin concluded that every serious mental illness can be placed into either one of two large categories: those involving a mood disorder (depression, mania, and anxiety) and those not associated with any mood disorder (cases then known as dementia praecox, later named schizophrenia). The patients with mood disorders were expected to improve with time, whereas those with schizophrenia were not. Kraepelin's introduction of a simple two-part classification enabled psychiatrists to discard a basketful of clinical disease labels that included such items as "masturbatory insanity," "wedding-night psychosis," and "chronic delusional disorder." The dichotomous scheme was truly useful and therefore widely adopted. Importantly, it began a shift of professional interest away from biology and toward psychology because Kraepelin had achieved his success not by laboring in the research laboratory but by conducting careful clinical observations.

The psychological version of the medical model was further advanced by Sigmund Freud (1856–1939). He was born in the same year as Emil Kraepelin, and, like Kraepelin, he immersed himself in German neuroscience as a young medical student. Later, of course, he radically changed his orientation (again like Kraepelin) by constructing a complex psychodynamic theory. He divided the mind into three parts: the id, the ego, and the superego. Further, he believed that much of the mind's emotionally charged material is processed unconsciously, so people are often unaware of the reasons for their behaviors. To overcome the potential or actual contribution of unconscious processes to pathological mental conditions, Freud invented psychoanalysis.

Freud had an enormous, but temporary, influence on psychiatry. By focusing so strongly on mental processes as the causes of personal malfunction, Freud drew attention to the psychological version of the medical model. Moreover, his influence was not limited to a closed circle of professionals. He and his followers also influenced large segments of the educated public to believe that mental illnesses are fundamentally psychological in nature. While the psychoanalytic craze has subsided from its peak in the first half of the twentieth century, Freud's ideas still hold a place in the public imagination. Indeed, the pursuit of psychological insight—broadly defined—is as popular now as ever before.

Although none of Freud's extensive writings contains an explicit discussion of mind–body philosophy, the overall conception is clearly dualistic. Interestingly, Freud's theoretical framework, involving a structured mind in which the various elements come into conflict with each other, is reminiscent of Plato. Both authors pit a higher mental component (Plato's reason, Freud's ego/superego) against a lower, more dangerous component (Plato's passion, Freud's id), and both see sickness stemming from the conflict, although the authors clearly differ on other points.[9] I am not suggesting that psychological explanations of mental processes and mental illness *necessarily* imply philosophical dualism. Psychological talk does not have to be talk about a mind thing or a mind substance. We will see, in Chapter 7, that psychological explanations are compatible with the philosophical view that mind is just a property of the brain. Nevertheless, for many people, psychological talk *does* reflect dualistic thinking.

Freud had a significant impact on my own life in the late 1950s, at a time when my elder brother was becoming ill with schizophrenia. The American Jewish community treated Freud with enormous respect, and so my family was well aware of his work.[10] It did not escape our notice that while Freud himself treated only neurotic patients, certain of his disciples applied his ideas to the problem of schizophrenia. For us, the writings of Frieda Fromm-Reichmann were especially damaging. Here is her description of what she called "the basic schizophrenic dynamics":

> The schizophrenic is painfully distrustful and resentful of other people, due to the severe early warp and rejection he encountered in important people of his infancy and childhood, as a rule, mainly in a schizophrenogenic mother . . . . The schizophrenic's partial emotional regression and his withdrawal from the outside world into an autistic private world with its specific thought processes and modes of feeling and expression is motivated by his fear of repetitional rejection, his distrust of others, and equally so by his own retaliative hostility, which he abhors, as well as the deep anxiety promoted by this hatred.[11]

In placing the blame for schizophrenia "mainly" on "schizophreno-genic mothers," rather than on genes, viruses, and birthing mishaps (as now believed), Fromm-Reichmann laid a heavy burden of guilt on many women, including my mother.

Some Say It's Not Even an Illness

Mental illness has probably been present, in one form or another, since the early days of human existence. Given its unusual features, one might expect a variety of interpretations, and that is indeed what history demonstrates. While many interpretations are born of dualistic assumptions, others are not. Ultimately, the choice of the "best" interpretation depends on one's philosophical and moral inclinations, which are inevitably shaped by time and location. The French historian, Michel Foucault, emphasizes this fact in his important book, *Madness and Civilization,*[12] in which he analyzes peoples' responses to "madness," as it was called in the years from 1500 to 1800. His main point is that while responses changed radically during this period, from indifference to fear and then punishment, the direction of the changes was always related to shifts in societal values. The mental derangements were the same, but their interpretations varied as social concerns varied. In other words, says Foucault, there is no essential nature of mental illness; it is invariably defined by society. This may well be true. However, as the philosopher Rachel Cooper points out, we have no alternative but to understand mental illness according to the values and assumptions present in the society in which we live.[13] Since science is today the dominant influence in advanced societies, I favor an interpretation based on scientific knowledge and monist philosophy.

Things were different even as recently as the 1960s. At that time, during the unpopular war in Vietnam, political rebellion combined with a celebration of personal freedom to create a climate hostile to psychiatry. Deviant behaviors were seen not as signs of illness, but as expressions of unconventional individuality. Hospitals and asylums were denounced as institutions of banishment where so-called medical treatments were not only ineffective but punitive. In sum, the anti-psychiatrists dismissed psychiatry as an instrument used to enforce socially defined standards of behavior. For them, the very notion of mental illness was nonsense.

Another thread in the antipsychiatry movement emphasized the claim that disease, by definition, requires evidence of a physical anomaly. Authors such as Christopher Boorse, mentioned above, argued that since no such evidence is present in patients said to be suffering from a mental illness, the conditions should not be described as medical. Thomas Szasz elaborated the point in his celebrated book, *The Myth of Mental Illness*.[14] The title already announces Szasz's alternative interpretation of mental illness. Using frank and provocative language, Szasz documents the weakness of the evidence for physical abnormalities. He combines this with the argument that individuals are labeled as mentally ill only if their behavior violates social or political norms. Thus, for him, as for the other antipsychiatrists, the myth of mental illness serves the social establishment. It is important to note, however, that Szasz's book was published in 1961, at the nadir of research in biological psychiatry. A lot has changed since then. In chapter 6, I review the more recent neuroscientific and genetic evidence that, beyond any reasonable doubt, proves the biological basis for the abnormal behaviors that are commonly referred to as mental illness.

Long before the twentieth-century antipsychiatrists dismissed mental illness as a myth, many earlier commentators likewise refused to call in the doctors. They too viewed deviant behavior through broadly moral lenses. An example of this point of view is found in the writings attributed to Homer, from about the first millennium BC. When human actors behave oddly in the *Illiad* and the *Odyssey*, it is because the gods have made them do it. Abnormal behavior is not a sign of illness, but evidence of a malevolent controller who is influencing people to commit morally repugnant acts. In some cases, men are manipulated by gods in order that one god can gain an advantage over another god. In other cases, the gods create "mad men" as punishments for their hubris.[15] However, while the earlier authors denigrated the deviants, at least Szasz and his fellow critics defended them.

Christianity has also tended to treat mental illness as a moral issue, and a serious one at that. Writing of the church's views in the fifth century AD, one historian of psychiatry asserts that "[t]he whole liturgical and dogmatic apparatus of the Church was designed to [deal with] mental diseases."[16] However, the victims were not treated as patients. The influential texts of St. Augustine (354–430) are replete with passages interpreting mental disturbances—usually characterized by excesses of passion—as evidence of sin. The church's way of dealing with these afflicted persons was to denounce and punish them. This type of response was especially prominent during the fifteenth, sixteenth, and early seventeenth centuries. Persons with mental troubles were held responsible for their conditions because it was assumed that they had succumbed to the evil influences of demons. To salvage their spiritual selves, cleanse the church, and make the community safe, these individuals were subjected to physical violence often leading to death.[17] As in Homer's epic poems, the disturbances are attributed not to causes *within* the individual, but to supernatural agents *outside* the individual. In Homer's case, it is a god; in the church's case, an evil spirit. In both perspectives, the troubled person has neither a psychological disorder nor a physical illness; rather, he or she has committed a moral transgression.

Public Opinion is Confused and Misinformed

Given its inherent perplexities, and recognizing the history of diverse interpretations, it is hardly surprising that a variety of contemporary views lies hidden beneath the conventional label, mental illness. Although the range of opinion is greater in the general population than among psychiatric professionals, it is striking to see that old ideas persist in one form or another in both populations. Many of the expressed attitudes reflect underlying dualistic assumptions, as will be evident in the data discussed below.

Several large-scale, formal surveys have addressed the question of how people think about mental illness. One well-designed survey of 1,444 Americans examined what people see as the *causes* of certain mental disorders.[18] The participants were first asked to read brief vignettes describing the symptoms exhibited by imaginary persons. Each vignette described a different illness or syndrome, and all vignettes were based on standard criteria established by the psychiatric community. Here, for example, is the vignette for schizophrenia; the bracketed terms were systematically varied for different respondents.

> John is a [ethnicity] man with an [level] education. Up until a year ago, life was pretty okay for John. But then, things started to change. He thought that people around him were making disapproving comments and talking behind his back. John was convinced that people were spying on him and that they could hear what he was thinking. John lost his drive to participate in this usual work and family activities and retreated to his home, eventually spending most of his day in his room. John was hearing voices even though no one else was around. These voices told him what to do and what to think. He has been living this way for six months.

Table 2.1 **The causes of psychiatric illness according to a large American survey**

	Major depressive disorder (percent)	Schizophrenia (percent)
Own bad character	38	33
Chemical imbalance in the brain	73	85
Way person was raised	48	45
Stressful circumstances in the person's life	95	91
Genetic or inherited problem	53	67
God's will	15	17

The percentages show the proportion of respondents who agreed with the indicated cause.

After a participant had read the vignette, he or she was asked, "In your opinion, how likely is it that John's situation might be caused by ...?" The choices are shown below together with the percentage of respondents choosing each one.

Several features of the results are noteworthy (see Table 2.1). First, the respondents identified a wide range of causes. Second, the causes, "own bad character" and "God's will," are credited by a significant fraction of the public, revealing either an ignorance of science or, more likely, a rejection of science. In either case, they signify an attitude based on moral concerns. Third, the credence given to the option, "chemical imbalance in the brain," is misdirected according to current science, although it may have been in line with popular conceptions at the time of polling (1996). Scientists now say that chemical imbalance is an overly simplified, inaccurate description of the chemical alterations found in the brains of mentally ill persons. If the option had stipulated "brain abnormalities" instead of chemical imbalance, the option would have merited 100 percent agreement.

A German survey used methods similar to those described above, but focused on schizophrenia.[19] The participants read vignettes describing behaviors typical of schizophrenia and then indicated what they thought were the causes. A stunning result was that 50 percent of respondents cited "lack of will power" as a cause of schizophrenia. When compared with the alternatives, "lack of will power" was chosen as a cause about as frequently as psychosocial stress, biological factors, and psychological factors. A different survey, conducted in the United States in 2008, shows that the public is poorly informed not only about the causes of schizophrenia, but also about its symptoms.[20] Most people correctly identified delusions and hallucinations as symptoms (80 percent and 79 percent, respectively), but the equally characteristic symptoms of thought disorganization and social withdrawal were less frequently identified (62 percent and 61 percent, respectively), and 64 percent of the respondents replied—incorrectly—that schizophrenia involves split or multiple personalities. Fifty-three percent of the respondents said that schizophrenia is *the same as* split personality disorder. Another 8 percent said that schizophrenia is equivalent to mental retardation.

A 2008 survey conducted for the Canadian Medical Association found that 46 percent of respondents agreed with the statement, "We call some things mental illness because it gives some people an excuse for their poor behavior and personal failings."[21] Also, 10 percent of respondents agreed with the statement, "Most people with mental illnesses could just snap out of it if they really wanted to." When asked "how familiar" they were with various health conditions, only 24 percent said that they were either extremely familiar or very familiar with schizophrenia, compared to 52 percent for depression, 52 percent for diabetes, 56 percent for cancer, and 38 percent for HIV/AIDS. Remarkably, HIV/AIDS is about four times *less prevalent* than schizophrenia, yet people are *more familiar* with HIV/AIDS than with schizophrenia. The discrepancy could be due to the large amount of publicity recently given to HIV/AIDS, but it may also suggest that schizophrenia is stigmatized to an even greater degree than HIV/AIDS.

The preceding surveys suggest not just a lack of knowledge, but also a proclivity for moral judgments and a reliance on dualistic assumptions. The influence of dualism is obvious in some of the data, for example in the striking finding that 50 percent of the German respondents cited "lack of will power" as a cause of schizophrenia, and in the 10 percent of Canadians who believe that "most people with mental illnesses could just snap out of it if they really wanted to." Apparently at odds with these results is the finding that roughly 85 percent of Americans believe "chemical imbalances" cause schizophrenia. I do not think that these several results reflect national differences of opinion. Rather, people can say one thing while believing something else, and no one is entirely consistent in his or her beliefs. Persons responding to polls will likely have been exposed to publicity or news stories featuring the neuroscience of mental illness. From this, they might sense an obligation to acknowledge a biological basis for mental illness. Even while complying with the expectation, however, these same individuals could harbor a tacit dualistic philosophy and, consequently, an implicit dualistic attitude toward mental illness. Their dualism might have been expressed if they had been asked about it, but they were not asked. In short, I suspect that many people have ambivalent attitudes about mental illness. A close examination of the results from the American survey (see Table 2.1) supports my conclusion. While the choice "chemical imbalance" gets the largest response, 85 percent, substantial percentages are also reported for several other possible causes, including 33 percent for "own bad character" and 15 percent for "God's will." Adding up all the percentage figures in the right-hand column, the total comes to 659 percent. This means that individual respondents entered multiple choices, thereby expressing a belief in multiple causes. Many people evidently think that schizophrenia is caused by "chemical imbalances" *and* "own bad character" *and/or* "God's will."

Dualistic Thinking in Psychiatry

The word *Psychiaterie* (later shortened to *Psychiatrie*) was first used by German physicians beginning in 1808. The term derives, of course, from the Greek word *psyche*, meaning mind. Thus, like Emily Brontë's *mental illness* (1847), the name of this new discipline references a psychological version of the medical model. Although dualism per se was not necessarily in the thoughts of those who promoted psychiatry in the nineteenth century, nor is it today the subject of much discussion in the specialty, the general idea of mind has always been central in the thinking of most practitioners. The medical historian, Roy Porter, recounts the course of events that brought mind to its position of prominence in psychiatry.

> The great upheavals of early modern times [roughly, the seventeenth and eighteenth centuries] had produced profound difficulties for conceptualizing the nature of personal identity and consciousness, and grasping their relations to the world in which people lived. Belief in a transcendental (Christian) soul was generally retained in eighteenth century discourse, but it ceased to be the medium through which daily life was conducted. Moreover,

19

as traditional humorism [bile and phlegm] waned, its associated language for mapping a self on to the body went by the wayside. Thus the links in the chain between mind and body grew less tangible; the more it was analyzed, the more intractable the mind/body problem became. And many features of late enlightenment thought made it attractive to refined elites to nurture ways of talking about personality in which the mark of true distinction lay in the cultivation of "mind," "soul" or "sensibility," viewed as distinct from the grossly corporal. The age of the "march of mind" was dawning; mind over matter was to become the new watchword.[22]

While the leading figures in the emerging field of psychiatry did not record their explicit philosophies of mind, it is known that they were influenced by the English philosopher, John Locke. Locke believed, as did Descartes, that the mind is distinct from the brain. In his theory of mind, he proposed that knowledge derives solely from sensory experience and that from sensations come ideas. Rational minds are able to associate two or more ideas to reach valid conclusions. Irrational minds, by contrast, make false associations and so create delusions and hallucinations. Locke's conjectures are particularly relevant for their influence on the two men most responsible for reforming psychiatry at the beginning of the nineteenth century, William Tuke and Philippe Pinel.[23]

To know the philosophical inclinations of psychiatrists today, we must turn to the few articles and books in which psychiatrists express themselves, since there are no formal surveys. It is telling that some professional leaders have recently spoken out against what they perceive as the widespread influence of dualist philosophies. Dr. Kenneth Kendler, for example, writing in the *American Journal of Psychiatry*, calls for a broad change of attitude. "It is time," he says, "for the field of psychiatry to declare that Cartesian substance dualism is false." He continues,

> This rejection of Cartesian dualism requires a significant shift in our way of thinking . . . dualistic thinking and vocabulary remain deeply entrenched in our approach to clinical and research problems. From the ways we organize our clinical presentations to our categorizations of risk factors, we remain deeply imbedded in the Cartesian framework of seeing the mind and brain as reflecting fundamentally different spheres of reality.[24]

Dr. Marc Miresco and Dr. Laurence Kirmayer also published an article in the *American Journal of Psychiatry*. Like Dr. Kendler, they lament the fact that "psychiatrists continue to operate dualistically in ways that are often covert and unacknowledged."[25] And, they have their own advice for colleagues, "Instead of assuming that medicine and psychiatry have transcended dualism, it may prove more useful for clinicians to acknowledge its continuing influence on their thinking and to consider carefully the potential implications of this kind of reasoning."[26] One notable "implication" of dualistic thinking, according to Drs. Miresco and Kirmayer, is that patients are likely to be blamed for their own illnesses, a situation that I discuss in chapter 4.

A fourth-year medical student became so upset with the negative attitudes of his psychiatric mentors that he wrote an editorial for a Web-based journal of the American Medical Association.[27] In the piece, Sam Huber expresses concern that his fellow students are turning away from psychiatry as a career choice because of outdated attitudes in the field. He urges his colleagues to adopt a more positive, more modern perspective on mental illness, and he identifies "Descartes' mind–body dichotomy" as one source of the profession's antiquated views.

As an alternative to dualism, a growing number of psychiatrists embrace empirical science and identify themselves as "biological psychiatrists." One leader of this movement, Dr. Eric Kandel, published a manifesto of sorts under the title, "A New Intellectual Framework for Psychiatry."[28] His first principle (among five) asserts, "All mental processes, even the most complex psychological processes, derive from operations of the brain . . . . [W]hat we commonly call mind is a range of functions carried out by the brain." Therefore, he concludes, "[B]ehavioral disorders that characterize psychiatric illness are disturbances of brain function." Kandel, together with his like-minded colleagues, promotes a nuanced version of monistic philosophy, which I will later describe in detail.

It should be noted that both popular and professional views about mental illness vary across cultures.[29] Because peoples' intuitions about the mind are also culturally specific,[30] a question arises as to whether the prevailing philosophies of mind influence conceptions of mental illness. In his illuminating study of this issue, the anthropologist and psychiatrist, Horatio Fabrega, quotes from Emil Kraepelin's historically important description of schizophrenia. According to Kraepelin, schizophrenia involves "the loss of the inner unity of thought, feeling and acting, the blunting of higher feelings, the manifold and peculiar disorders of the will with their associated delusion of the loss of psychic freedom and influences, [and] finally, the disintegration of the personality . . . ."[31] Fabrega states that Kraepelin's description of schizophrenia emphasizes a concept of the self that is typically Western European and Anglo-American, and less common elsewhere. The main features of the self in Western psychiatric literature are "its inner mentalistic constitution, its composition into tangible properties that govern and characterize subjectivity and behavior, and its capacity to be altered and disturbed/destroyed by the 'schizophrenia' that enters the self."[32] From this, we may conclude that the Western concept of the self is strongly tied to dualism. Hence, Westerners are likely to see illnesses that affect the sense of self as illnesses affecting the mind. Schizophrenia, at least in the Western conception, is a disorder of the mind.[33]

Summary and Forward Glance

From every perspective—historical, statistical, and personal—I see people struggling to understand mental illness. The nature of the condition forces us to think about the mind and the body. We are led to wonder whether persons who behave strangely are sick or just deviant, whether there is a problem in the mind or in the brain, or perhaps in both the mind and the brain. The survey data summarized above indicate that public attitudes reflect many of the same differences of opinion that were present in previous times, some going back nearly to the beginning of written history. Public knowledge of the symptoms and causes of the major mental illnesses is patchy at best, and no doubt confounded by indecision over whether to consider these disorders in biological, psychological, or social terms. Moreover, psychiatric professionals are not without their own confusions and not necessarily more sophisticated in their viewpoints.

Clouding the entire problem of interpretation, in my opinion, is a misconception regarding the nature of mind. This does not affect the assumption that mental illness is indeed an illness, which is widely accepted, but rather it weighs on the perceived locus of the illness. Crucially, the philosophy of dualism allows the possibility that the illness is in the mind, and a literal, grammatical reading of the term *mental illness* sustains this point of view. Alternatively, if we decide that there is no mind distinct and separate from the body, then one can reasonably conclude that the illness is in the brain. The difference between these interpretations—in the mind or in the body—is important because it affects our attitudes toward mentally ill persons, the choice of treatments, and ultimately, the understanding of ourselves as human beings.

In the next chapter, I will describe dualism more fully, explain its origins, and expose its weaknesses. I will also give evidence for my conclusion that most people are probably dualists at heart. We need to understand the attraction of dualism before we can tackle its negative effects, which will be further described in chapter 4.

Notes

1. Kudlien, 1962.
2. Boorse, 1975; Jennings, 1986.
3. Cooper, 2007, chapter 3.
4. Boorse, 1975.
5. Cooper, 2007, p. 42.
6. Hippocrates, *On the Sacred Disease*, http://classics.mit.edu/Hippocrates/sacred.html.
7. See chapter 6.
8. For a full account, see Shorter, 1997.
9. Simon, 1978, pp. 200–15, compares and contrasts the two theories.
10. For a discussion of Freud's influence in America, see Shorter, 1997, pp. 181–89.
11. Fromm-Reichmann, 1948, p. 265.
12. Foucault, 1965.
13. Cooper, 2007, pp. 14–6.
14. Szasz, 1961.
15. Another reason why mental illness has no place in Homer is because his human characters seem to have no minds! I return to this point in the next chapter.
16. Roccatagliata, 1986, p.74.
17. Zilboorg, 1941.
18. Link et al., 1999.
19. Angermeyer and Matschinger, 1994.
20. Harris/NAMI survey, http://www.nami.org/sstemplate.cfm?section=SchizophreniaSurvey.
21. National Report Card on Health Care, http://www.cma.ca/multimedia/CMA/Content_Images/Inside_cma/Annual_Meeting/2008/GC_Bulletin/National_Report_Card_EN.pdf.
22. Porter, 1987, pp. 281–82.
23. For more on Tuke and Pinel, see p. 53.
24. Kendler, 2005, p. 434.
25. Miresco and Kirmayer, 2006, pp. 913.
26. Ibid., p. 917–18.
27. Huber, S. Stigma, society, and specialty choice: What's going on? *Virtual Mentor* 5, no. 10, 2003, http://virtualmentor.ama-assn.org/2003/10/medu1-0310.html.
28. Kandel, 1998. See Chapter 7 for further discussion of this paper.
29. Littlewood, 1998.

30. Innateness and the structure of the mind project, http://www.philosophy.
     dept.shef.ac.uk/AHRB-Project/.
31. Quoted in Fabrega, 1989, p. 280.
32. Fabrega, 1989, p. 281.
33. In Asia, schizophrenia is likewise understood as an illness of the mind,
     although not necessarily an assault on the self. See Kim and Berrios, 2001,
     and my summary of their analysis on p. 58.

3

Descartes' Dualism

Given the unusual characteristics of mental illness, one's perspective on the condition is necessarily tied up with the philosophical conundrum known as the mind–body problem. I believe that most people are dualists and that is why they interpret the term mental illness literally, not metaphorically. Dualism is an old philosophy that retains a strong appeal despite its flaws. To understand its appeal, we must examine its substance, its history, and its resonance in human nature. All of these factors combine to explain why dualistic interpretations of mental illness persist even as the evidence of biological causation accumulates.

Although dualism is widely accepted, it is by no means the only possible philosophy of mind, as we will learn in chapter 5. Some philosophers, but few ordinary folk, even dismiss as nonsense the whole notion of mind. For most people, however, the mind is an inescapable aspect of human existence that begs an explanation of one sort or another. Moreover, people talk a lot about the mind. This fact has been verified by a team of British scholars, which analyzed an electronic databank comprising one hundred million words that had been either spoken or written.[1] They found that the noun *mind* was said 164 times per one million *spoken* words, ranking it 532 in a total of about one million English words. In *written* text, *mind* appeared 219 times per one million words, for rank 435. These data come from the analysis of all spoken and written words, thus including verbs, articles, adjectives, etc. When only nouns were analyzed, with spoken and written words combined, *mind* ranked 130. From these results, we may fairly conclude that *mind* is often on, or in, the mind.

What are people talking about when they talk about the mind? Everyone uses expressions such as those copied below. Simple and everyday though they are, each reveals something about the common concept of mind.

"I have a *mind* to . . . ."
"It's all in his *mind*."
"John is out of his *mind*."
"Larry has lost his *mind*."
"Marilyn has a brilliant *mind*."
"Henry has a dirty *mind*."

These expressions show that people speak about the mind as if it were a *thing*, an entity possessed by themselves and others. We also see that this thing, the mind, can have certain *qualities*, some good, some bad. Finally, there is the suggestion that the mind is a *vessel* that contains *stuff*. To further investigate properties of the mind, I ask you to participate in a little exercise. Just put down this book, close your eyes, and think, *what is in my mind?* Open your eyes from time to time to write down the things that are in your mind. Stop reading now and actually do it. Once you have compiled a short list, return here for further reading.

If you are reading this, you have already done the exercise. Look at your notes. You might have written down something about the concept of mind, the pain in your back, or the dog barking. Possibly, you had a notion to ignore this book and get on with the laundry. Whatever it is that you wrote down, I imagine that your consciousness shifted frequently from one thought or feeling to another thought or feeling. It is unlikely that your mind was *empty* because, for most people most of the time, there is *something on the mind*. That is all the exercise was intended to demonstrate.

Philosophers use the same everyday expressions as everyone else, so presumably they share the same, or similar, intuitions. Indeed, while the philosophers disagree about many issues relating to the mind, they generally agree on what it is that they are talking *about*. Philosophers think of mind as possessing two special properties, *subjectivity* and *intentionality*. Subjectivity obviously includes consciousness, and it also includes the somewhat different experience of self-consciousness, when we focus awareness on our own consciousness. Mind, therefore, makes possible our sense of self. Besides consciousness, philosophers have a special fondness for the qualitative aspect of subjectivity that is associated with perceptions, emotions, and bodily sensations. Collectively, these phenomena are known as *qualia*. We experience qualia when, for example, we taste a pineapple, smell urine, jump into the salty ocean water, or hear a low note bowed on a cello. Owing to the special something associated with each quale, the qualia as a whole are workhorses in philosophical debate, as we will see. Turning now to the mental phenomena that philosophers refer to as intentional, these are the states of mind that are *about* something or someone. Intentional states, therefore, include loving, hoping, wanting, and thinking. As a technical term in philosophy, intentionality covers much more than mere intending. It roughly corresponds to the notion of meaning. Some philosophers say that intentionality is the very essence of the mental, that everything mental is about something.

Dualism Before Descartes

Dualist thinking is already evident in the flaky papyrus scrolls, collectively known as the *Book of the Dead*, which were written in ancient Egypt about 1,500 BC. The scrolls were intended for people in their afterlives, and they speak of spells and instructions. A dualistic element is evident in the distinction drawn between the physical person and the six distinct parts of the soul. They identify the most important part of the soul as *Ib*, meaning heart. The Egyptians understood *Ib* to be the seat of emotions, thoughts, and volitions. For this reason, the *Book of the Dead* prescribes that the heart of a deceased must be preserved by embalming, while the brain tissue is to be sucked out through the nostrils and destroyed. (So much for any part of the soul that may have resided in the brain!) Three other parts of the soul— *Ba* (personality), *Ka* (life force), and *Akh* (the effective one)—were understood to be immortal. It was assumed that they would survive the death of the body to continue in the afterlife. Rounding out the incorporeal parts of the person are the *Sheut* (shadow) and the *Ren* (name). Although the precise interpretation of each mind-like entity remains the subject of debate, it appears that the ancient Egyptians believed that humans comprise two distinct parts: material bodies and immaterial souls.

A stone monument, or stele, discovered in southeastern Turkey in 2008 bears additional evidence of ancient dualist thinking in the eighth century BC. Its inscription reads in part, "I, Kuttamuwa, servant of [the king] Panamuwa, am the one who oversaw the production of this stele for myself while still living. I . . . established a feast at this chamber [which included among other things] a ram for my soul that is in this stele."[2] According to the archaeologists who made the discovery, the find is important because it provides "the first written evidence that the people in this region held to the religious concept of the soul apart from the body." Moreover, the peoples of the region came to their dualism independently, or at least it does not appear that they were directly influenced by Egyptian culture.

The philosophical authors of the classical period in Greece seem to have gotten their dualism by way of the Orphic branch of the religion devoted to Bacchus (also known as Dionysus). The Orphic doctrines originated in Egypt and were transmitted to Greece via Crete around 3,000 BC.[3] Orpheus was either an actual person, an imaginary hero, or a god. Like Bacchus, Orpheus was also fond of intoxication, but rather than achieving the state through alcohol, he preferred cerebral or spiritual methods. Music eventually became his main inspiration and his favored route to intoxication, but early in life he practiced asceticism. His followers believed in the transmigration of souls, meaning the passage of the soul after death into another body.

Anaxagoras (500?–428 BC) was the first author to explicitly write about the mind as an abstract concept and something to be distinguished from matter.[4] Mind first created the physical world, he said, and then it entered into all living things. He wrote that mind is infinite and independent and that it has power over all life-forms. Anaxagoras is important as an historical precedent, but his influence was limited by his low literary output. On the other hand, Plato, born just before the death of Anaxagoras, was a prolific author.

Plato's huge influence on the development of modern dualism derives largely from his dialogue *Phaedo*. In this work, Socrates lays out his ideas on life and death just before drinking a fatal concoction of hemlock. Here, the Orphic religion is fully transformed into an ascetic philosophy. The soul is distinct from the body, and only the soul is immortal. Socrates argues that people should devote themselves to the cultivation of the soul, while avoiding the distracting pleasures (and pains) of the body. The focus of one's life should be the acquisition of knowledge through pure thought. Because the body can hamper one's attempt to gain knowledge, death can be a blessing. In the following passage, Socrates sums up his views on the body and the soul, as related by Plato.

> [A]ll experience shows that if we would have pure knowledge of anything we must be quit of the body, and the soul in herself must behold all things in themselves: then I suppose that we shall attain that which we desire, and of which we say that we are lovers, and that is wisdom, not while we live, but after death, as the argument shows;

for if while in company with the body the soul cannot have pure knowledge, one of two things seems to follow—either knowledge is not to be attained at all, or, if at all, after death. For then, and not till then, the soul will be in herself alone and without the body. In this present life, I reckon that we make the nearest approach to knowledge when we have the least possible concern or interest in the body . . . .[5]

Plato's student, Aristotle (384–322 BC), was not a strong dualist, and perhaps not a dualist at all. Nevertheless, his views played an important role in the advancement of dualism because they influenced the medieval Christian theologian, Thomas Aquinas. In his book *De Anima* (On the Soul), Aristotle wrote obscurely of the soul as the principle of life.[6] He asserted that the soul is the logical essence of the body but, contrary to Plato, he did not clearly state that the soul is incorporeal and immortal. In much of his writing, he seems to express a metaphysics similar to that of modern materialist philosophers. Interestingly though, Aristotle made an exception for the *nous*, which he understood to be a special part of the soul concerned with truth. In certain passages of *De Anima*, he seems to suggest that the *nous*, in contrast to other parts of the soul, is immaterial and survives the death of the body. Thomas Aquinas (1225–74) used this small, uncertain concession as the basis for his belief in the resurrection of the body. Here is a passage from his most significant book, *Summa Theologica*:

> Therefore the intellectual principle, called the mind or the intellect, does act on its own account and independent [sic] of the body. But nothing can act on its own account unless it subsists in its own right. For there is no acting save in actuality: hence in as much as something acts it exists. Which is why we do not say that heat, but the hot object, heats. The conclusion, is, therefore, that the human soul, which is called the mind or intellect, is something incorporeal and subsistent.[7]

Aquinas says that the mind and the soul are the same and that both are incorporeal. Elsewhere he wrote that if the soul is incorporeal, it must also be immortal; the persistence of the soul after the death of the body allows for the resurrection of the body. Aquinas had a huge influence on Christian theology. René Descartes, who studied at a Jesuit college and remained respectful of the church throughout his life, was surely introduced to Aquinas's ideas at an early age. In any event, Descartes arrived at a concept of the mind, or soul, that bears a strong resemblance to the one espoused by Aquinas four centuries earlier.

Dualism According to Descartes

Although he had dualist predecessors, the name most closely associated with metaphysical dualism is René Descartes. No book ever written has had a greater impact on popular conceptions of the mind than his *Discourse on the Method*, published in 1637. Exceptional in its time, the *Discourse* delved deeply into the nature of consciousness. The literary style was also unusual. While most of his contemporaries were writing in Latin, a language that was rapidly becoming obsolete, Descartes wrote in French, the language of the masses. Moreover, he pitched his arguments in an accessible, fresh voice. In a letter to a friend, Descartes declared that he intentionally wrote in a style that could be understood *even by women*! Finally, his enthusiasm for new knowledge meshed perfectly with the cultural renaissance that was then sweeping across Europe. All together, these features made for compelling reading. Although the *Discourse on the Method* was intended as the preface to a trio of essays on scientific subjects, the *Discourse* itself is highly philosophical in content. In this book and elsewhere, Descartes uses the word *l'âme*, which ordinarily translates as the soul, but since his concept of the soul is close to our contemporary concept of the mind, I will use both words interchangeably in discussing his works.

Descartes was obsessed with finding the truth. He cared, of course, about *what* is true, but he also cared, deeply, about *how one can be sure* that something is true. He was troubled, for example, by the realization that a person can be easily deceived about reality. Thus, he wrote of his dreams, in which he would think that he was sitting beside his fireplace when, in fact, he was lying in bed. Rationalizing from such experiences, Descartes comes to the famous conclusion,

> I noticed that, while I was trying to think that everything was false, it was necessary that I, who was thinking this, should be something. And observing that this truth: *I think, therefore I am,* was so firm and secure that all the most extravagant suppositions of the skeptics were not capable of overthrowing it, I judged that I should not scruple to accept it as the first principle of the philosophy that I was seeking.[8]

For those who prefer Latin, the italicized phrase in the passage translates as *Cogito, ergo sum,* or simply *Cogito,* the name by which it is known in philosophical discourse. Descartes may well have picked up the idea from Saint Augustine, who wrote something similar more than twelve centuries earlier. The emphasis on *thinking* should not be considered limiting because from other passages, it is clear that Descartes understood the word to mean the same as our modern word *consciousness,* that is, as encompassing feelings, beliefs, intentions, images, etc. Thus, an alternative reading of the *Cogito* is, "I am conscious, therefore I am." Immediately following the *Cogito* statement, the *Discourse* continues with a declaration concerning personal identity. As we read these sentences today, nearly 400 years after they were written, Descartes still strikes an intuitive chord.

> Then, examining with attention what I was, and seeing that I could pretend that I had no body, and that there was no world, nor any place in which I was; but that I could not pretend, for all that, that I did not exist; and that, on the contrary, from the very fact that I could think of doubting the truth of other things, it followed very evidently and certainly that I existed; whereas, if I had only ceased to think, even if all the rest of what I had imagined were true, I should not have had any reason to believe that I existed; I knew from that that I was a substance whose whole essence or nature is only that of thinking, and which, in order to exist, has no need of any place, nor depends on any material thing. Thus this "I", that is to say the soul by which I am what I am, is entirely distinct from the body. . . .[9]

Descartes' dualism is starkly evident in the final sentence quoted above, "the soul . . . is entirely distinct from the body . . . ." He asserts that his soul is a *substance* that "has no need of any place, nor depends on any material thing." Only humans have souls, he writes elsewhere, whereas animals are pure machines. Why does Descartes refer to the soul as a substance? Following Aquinas's use of the same word (note the words *subsists* and *subsistent* in the passage quoted above from *Summa Theologica*), substance had become a jargon term for things that are independent of other things. Indeed, Descartes believed that the soul is absolutely independent from everything else in the universe, with the exception of God. The soul is real. It is a thing; hence, it is a substance. He further explains the meaning of substance in this excerpt from his *Principles of Philosophy.*

By substance, we can understand nothing else than a thing which so exists that it needs no other thing in order to exist. And in fact only one single substance can be understood which clearly needs nothing else, namely, God. We perceive that all other things can exist only by the help of the concourse of God . . . . Created substances, however, whether corporeal or thinking, may be conceived under this common concept; for they are things which need only the concurrence of God in order to exist.[10]

Some people have the notion that mind refers only to the contents of our consciousness, but Descartes was convinced that the mind is a special kind of entity. One modern authority expands on this idea, "[T]he mind is not just a collection of thoughts, but is *that which* thinks, an immaterial substance over and above its immaterial states."[11] Hence, Descartes' brand of metaphysics is known as *substance dualism.*

To explain the relationship of mind to body, Descartes wrote, "[W]e cannot by any means conceive a half or a third of a soul, nor what space it occupies, and . . . it is not diminished by the amputation of some part of the body, but separates itself from it as a whole when the union of the organs of the body is dissolved [i.e., at death]."[12] Also, in the *Discourse*, he declares that the soul is not "lodged in the human body like a pilot in a ship—except perhaps in order to move its limbs—but it is necessary for it to be joined and united more closely with the body, if it is to have feelings and desires like ours, and thus to constitute a true man."[13] Interestingly, both Aristotle and Thomas Aquinas had previously used the same "pilot in a ship" metaphor. For all three authors, the pilot in a ship is a counterexample. The mind, by contrast, does not simply *use* the body, nor is it an unfeeling accessory; the mind and the body are (somehow) intimately joined.

Descartes addresses the important issue of interactions between the immaterial mind and the physical brain. His answer is that the mind and the brain enjoy two-way interactions, that is, the brain can affect the mind and the mind can affect the brain. To the disappointment of his readers, however, Descartes expends little effort in defending this position. Perhaps he felt it unnecessary to say much because he knew that the idea accords well with our intuitions. In any case, he went further by boldly proposing an exact location where the mind and the brain interact. That place, he said, is the pineal gland. He based his speculation on the fact that the pineal gland lies near the center of the brain and is one of the few brain structures that is not bilaterally represented, that is not present in both hemispheres. While preposterous from the perspective of today's science, Descartes' promotion of the tiny pineal gland to such a prominent role can be appreciated as an imaginative attempt to link the disciplines of philosophy and neuroscience.[14]

Earlier, I characterized Descartes' philosophy of mind as substance dualism. We are now in a position to be even more precise, for we can say that Descartes advocated *interactive substance dualism*. More conveniently, we can simply call it *Cartesian dualism*. The latter label can be useful when one wishes to distinguish Descartes' particular ideas from other versions of dualism.[15] However, in the remainder of this book, whenever I mention dualism without qualification, it will be Cartesian dualism of which I speak; exceptions will be noted.

Stripped of its rhetoric, two ideas lie at the heart of Cartesian dualism: (1) the mind and the brain are separate entities, and (2) the mind is able to control the brain. Descartes convinced many people of the truthfulness of these ideas in seventeenth century Europe, but how do we react to them today? Who among us is a dualist? Are you? I think that *nearly everyone* is a dualist, and I intend to convince you that this is so.

Intuitions

Naively, I thought that it would be easy to find polling data to confirm that most people are dualists. All that would be required is to ask a random sample of people whether they believe that the mind is an entity and, if so, whether they think that it can control the brain. However, an extensive search for surveys of this type yielded only a single relevant study, and this one is flawed. I do not know why there has been just this one poll on the mind–body question. It is possible that pollsters find the issue impertinent or uninteresting, or maybe they are unable to frame good questions. In any case, I can briefly summarize the lone study that contains relevant data.[16] Two investigators asked 251 American college students to indicate the extent to which they believed in sixty statements relating to mind and body. The statements were of the type, "I no more choose my actions than the moon chooses to travel in a path around the earth," and "The human mind affects my actions, yet it is not some unique principle or reality distinct from the body." From the responses to sixty such statements, the investigators inferred the theory of mind held by each respondent. The results showed that dualism was the most popular theory. In the words of the study's authors, "Mind is not a function of the brain and it is not a metaphor. Mind exists simultaneously with the body."

A single survey result is indicative but hardly definitive, especially considering that this particular study used an unusual methodology, had a small sample size, and only questioned students at a now-defunct, church-related college. Unfortunately, there are no other poll results that might better reflect the views of the larger society. Therefore, to support my claim about the prevalence of dualism, I turn to other types of evidence, starting with the evidence of intuition.

Cartesian dualism makes intuitive sense; it seems so *obvious* that it just *must* be right. For example, I decide that I will move my hand in a precise manner—up, down, sideways—and then, whenever I am ready, I do it. Obviously, a thought in my mind commands the movement in my hand. The anthropologist Pascal Boyer is equally impressed with this demonstration, and, more to the point, he is in a position to confirm that people around the world think that willing the hand to move is an example of mind directing the body. Or, at very least, he assures us that people in English pubs and in the Fang villages of Cameroon believe this to be true because he personally interviewed them.[17] Boyer points out that it is only philosophers and cognitive scientists who are troubled by this apparent example of mind over matter; everybody else simply takes it for granted.

People ordinarily use mental terms, not brain terms, to explain behaviors. They say, "She cried out in *disappointment* because she *thought* that her husband no longer *trusted* her," not "She cried out because stellate cells in her left temporal lobe and right parietal lobe fired synchronously in 40 Hz bursts of activity and caused a rapid depolarization of Area 4a pyramidal neurons." We use unscientific, intuitive concepts in our everyday conversations to account for human behaviors. Scholars say that we employ a *folk psychology*.[18] We use folk psychology to explain, and in many cases even to predict, the actions of friends, coworkers, and strangers. Our use of folk psychology is significant because it carries the tacit assumption that people have minds and that minds cause behaviors.

Philosophers and cognitive psychologists suppose that our folk psychology is based on an unconscious *theory of mind* that contains enough principles of human behavior and rules of causation to account for behavior.[19] The theory of mind is itself only a theory because it is known only by its effects, principally our intuitive ability to understand human behaviors. Its language is that of everyday conversations, using terms such as *intention, hope,* and *wish,* rather than the terms of brain science. Because real advantages follow from the ability to predict other peoples' behaviors, it is easy to see how the theory of mind might have evolved. I stress, however, that I have not invoked folk psychology and the theory of mind to prove that mental events and mental states cause bodily actions; this is a deep philosophical issue to which I will return later. I am only saying that our common, everyday language implies a belief in minds.

If there is indeed a theory of mind, who or what possesses it? You might reply, "Well, I certainly possess a theory of mind." But what is the *I* of which you speak? Most people have a notion of their *selves* as something different from their bodies. It is I, myself, that has possessions, a reputation, a biography; it is not my body. The same attitude makes it reasonable to say, "I have a headache" or "I have a brain," expressions that would make no sense unless one thought of his/her self as separate from his/her body. This would also explain why a philosopher and a neurophysiologist coauthored a book with the curious title, *The Self and its Brain.*[20] Our intuition tells us that the self thinks, plans, believes, feels, etc. Thus, the self is understood as having similar functions as the mind. The closeness of the concepts *self* and *mind* explains why Plato wrote of the incorporeal soul as if it were synonymous with the person, and why Descartes used the word *l'âme* to designate that which philosophers and ordinary folk now call the mind. Because we think of the mind in the same way that we think of the self, I conclude that most of us who believe in the self also believe in the mind.

We tend to see minds at work everywhere around us, not only in our fellow humans, but also in our pets and even in inanimate objects. We love our pets, and we expect them to love us. When pet owners talk to their beloved four-legged animals, they ignore Descartes' insistence that only humans have minds. When our dog sulks or becomes aggressive, we bring it to a pet psychologist. If our car battery fails on a cold winter morning, we plead with it to start and, failing that, we curse it. Computers, too. When our computer crashes, we are as likely to blame *it* as we are to blame Bill Gates.

A classic laboratory experiment demonstrates our inclination to assign mental attributes to inanimate things. Fritz Heider and Mary-Ann Simmel constructed animated films featuring simple geometric shapes such as squares and circles that moved in a manner suggesting interactions between human actors.[21] Sure enough, when the subjects were questioned about the movies, they spoke of the shapes as autonomous agents responsible for their own actions. Moreover, they assumed that the shapes had mental properties appropriate for their roles in the imagined dramas. In one example, squares were seen as *bullies* beating up on circles; in other cases, shapes were described as *wanting* something or *intending* something. The participants attributed human-like mental properties to animated, but lifeless, shapes.

Paul Bloom, a psychologist at Yale University, has studied the process by which children learn about the mind. In his fascinating book, *Descartes' Baby*,[22] he describes how children distinguish living things from nonliving things, mental images from physical objects. Because the studies cited by Bloom mostly concern children who have not yet been exposed to either formal education or explicit philosophical instruction, they reveal the innate aspects of intuition. In one study, David Estes and colleagues addressed questions to children as young as three years old.[23] The children were told about three types of entities: real objects (such as a deflated balloon), real hidden objects (a deflated balloon inside a box), and mental images (an image of a deflated balloon); for the mental images, the children were instructed to close their eyes and told to "make a picture of it in your head." The children were then asked which of the three balloons, if any, they could stretch out and make skinny "just by thinking about it." Obviously, only the imagined balloon can be transformed just by thinking about it, and that is exactly what the three-year-olds said. From this experiment, and others like it, Estes and colleagues concluded,

> Preschool children in these studies consistently judge that mental phenomena—thoughts, memories, dreams, and mental images— differ in fundamental ways from physical phenomena . . . . [They] also frequently gave cogent and appropriate explanations for their correct responses . . . . This research further demonstrates that preschool children can apply their understanding of the mental- physical distinction to themselves and to others, can take their own mental experiences as objects of reflection and discourse, have at least a rudimentary capacity to transform mental images, and un- derstand the distinction between mental representation and what it represents.

In Paul Bloom's learned opinion, after reviewing many experimental studies such as the one described above, "People see bodies and souls as separate; we are common-sense dualists."[24] Moreover, he is able to claim support for his conclusion from a report written by the President's Council on Bioethics. This organization was convened by President George W. Bush to advise the president on issues of public concern. Its membership comprised a group of distinguished medical doctors, PhD's, and other intellectuals. In 2003, the Council issued a report under the title, *Being Human*, in which it proclaimed, "[W]e have both corporeal and noncorporeal aspects. We are embodied spirits and inspirited bodies, (or, if you will, embodied minds and minded bodies)."

Another author who has thought deeply about the mind and the brain is Michael Gazzaniga, a distinguished psychologist and neuroscientist. When asked by a radio show host to explain his views on the mind, he put it this way:

> Even though you know my brain is talking to you and that your brain is listening to me, we have this thing where no, I'm talking to Natasha and you're talking to Mike. I don't sit here and say, boy she has a cerebellum, wow, her left cortex is unbelievable, you know. You immediately treat the other entity as a person. We are all dualists, we immediately convert the biological reality of ourselves to personhood, to the fact that we're talking to people, not brains.[25]

Dualism in Contemporary Culture

So far, I have used polling data and intuition to infer what people think about the mind. Human culture provides an additional source of information. Paul Bloom discovered that even the entertainment industry offers telltale signs of implicit dualism. Here are some examples provided by Bloom to readers of the *New York Times*:

> Our dualism makes it possible for us to appreciate stories where people are liberated from their bodies. In the movie *13 Going on 30*, a teenager wakes up as Jennifer Garner, just as a 12-year-old was once transformed into Tom Hanks in *Big*. Characters can trade bodies, as in *Freaky Friday*, or battle for control of a single body, as when Steve Martin and Lily Tomlin fight it out in *All of Me*. Body-hopping is not a Hollywood invention. Franz Kafka tells of a man who wakes up one morning as a gigantic insect. Homer, writing hundreds of years before the birth of Christ, describes how the companions of Odysseus were transformed into pigs—but their minds were unchanged, and so they wept.[26]

Bloom's insight enables him to find evidence of dualism in other unexpected places. For example, consider this sentence at the end of a chapter in his book, "If you are in a bind and need to make a two-year-old laugh, the best way to do so is to adopt a surprised expression and fall on your ass."[27] What, you ask, has *this* got to do with dualism? Bloom contends that acts such as falling on your ass for no good reason are funny if and only if they draw on the contrast between mind and body. They are funny because they show a sensitive, feeling person trapped in an awkward, mechanical body. In effect, says Bloom, all slapstick comedy is based on philosophical dualism. And Bloom, an expert on child development, is quick to note that even two-year-olds are capable of appreciating good slapstick.

Psychoanalytic themes also contribute to jokes on occasion, but more importantly, the public's familiarity with Freudian ideas points to a fascination with mind, and it hints at dualism. The concept of *unconscious conflict* provides a good illustration of Freud's continuing influence with a public that has become largely ignorant of his actual work. In its original formulation, the concept applied to conflicts between instinctual drives and external realities. Later, Freud wrote of unconscious conflicts among parts of the mind, that is, among the id, the ego, and the superego. In a recent survey involving more than 5,000 German participants, 60 percent of the respondents agreed that unconscious conflict is a cause of schizophrenia, while 69 percent said that it is a cause of major depression.[28] As surprising as these results are, even more remarkable was the finding that only 2 percent of the respondents were able to provide a description of unconscious conflict that bore even a reasonable resemblance to Freud's definition. The organizers of the survey wrote that the respondents must have recognized the catchword phrase "unconscious conflict" and automatically assumed that it was involved in schizophrenia and major depression even though they did not understand what it meant. Casual references to psychoanalytic notions indicate an intuitive acceptance of dualism.

Religion provides further evidence that human cognition is predisposed toward dualism. About 3.4 billion people identify with one or another of the world's three major religions (Judaism, Christianity, and Islam), and all of these faiths, as well as a majority of the tribal religions, believe in supernatural entities, known as gods. Two large polls taken in 2008 reported figures of 93 percent (Gallup[29]) and

88 percent (Pew[30]) for the percentage of Americans believing in either a god or a "universal spirit." These are staggering numbers.

Dualists and the religious faithful share the belief in an immaterial (nonphysical) entity. For dualists, that entity is the mind distinct from the body; for the religious faithful, it is the supernatural being. Given the common ground, it is reasonable to imagine that individuals who believe in God also believe in the Cartesian mind. Therefore, given that a large majority of the population believes in God (according to the polls), one may conclude that most people believe in dualism.

The link between religious beliefs and dualistic beliefs is further illustrated by a recent empirical study.[31] The work revealed that, contrary to religious orthodoxy, which typically describes God as omnipresent (being everywhere at once) and omniscient (knowing everything), the religiously faithful implicitly assume that their gods have human-like qualities. It was demonstrated, for example, that people expect their gods to travel sequentially from one place to another and to rely on ordinary human-like senses to learn things. Thus, it appears that people in diverse cultures (not just North America) imagine their gods as very much like themselves, or as Voltaire wrote in the eighteenth century, "If God has made us in his image, we have returned him the favor." God is like ourselves except, of course, that he is immaterial. Thus, the common conception of God is that of a conscious, intentional entity with no body. In other words, God is like mind.

Gods and other supernatural beings are generally absent from Buddhist thought, but Buddhism cultivates an awareness of consciousness. The Buddha himself allegedly said, "There is nothing in the world but mind itself."[32] Jack Kerouac, the American poet and author of *On the Road*, was strongly attracted to both Catholicism and Buddhism, and he apparently conflated the two. Also, according to his biographer, Kerouac used the words *mind* and *God* interchangeably.[33]

Generally speaking, every person interested in spirituality or engaged in practices founded on spirituality is a person inclined to believe in dualism. The English word *spirit* comes from the Latin *spiritus*, which in ancient times meant *breath* as well as courage and strength. In current usage, a spirit is understood to be a transcendent, supernatural being. Spirituality can refer to the soul, to God, to a ghost, or to a universal consciousness. Indeed, the vagueness of its referents may contribute to the strong contemporary interest in spiritual beliefs and practices, among which are organized religions, astrology, meditation, yoga, magic, the occult, esotericism, mysticism, faith healing, I Ching, and certain of the martial arts. Regardless of the context, spirituality engages a belief in immaterial entities.

Everyone who has experienced Halloween Day in North America knows the popularity of ghosts. Confirming the impression, formal polling indicates that about one-half of all Americans either believe in ghosts or are "not sure" about them.[34] The anthropologist Pascal Boyer says that "the souls of the dead or their 'shadows' or 'presence' are the most widespread kind of supernatural agent the world over."[35] Still greater numbers of people believe in the afterlife. Polls conducted in the United States during the years from 1940 to 2008 found that 74–85 percent of respondents express a belief in life after death.[36] The numbers are similar for all religions—Catholic, Protestant, Jewish, and Muslim—but what is especially interesting is that, even for those who profess "no religion," a surprising 63 percent believe in an afterlife. This last statistic shows that although theological teachings may include statements about life after death, and even though such doctrines may act as inducements for those not yet initiated in a religion, the belief in an afterlife is *independent* of religious adherence. Indeed, there are reasons to think that the belief in an afterlife rests more on intuitive dualism than on religious faith.

Pascal Boyer emphasizes the ambivalent feelings evoked by dead bodies.[37] On the one hand, there is the unpleasant prospect of bodily decay and disease, which motivates the survivors to get rid of the body. On the other hand, mourners feel disinclined or unable to say goodbye to *the person* who inhabited the body, meaning the loving, thoughtful, and *good soul* that is Uncle David or Sister Joan. Boyer writes, "We are angry at dead people, we approve of what they did, scold them for having done this or that and very often resent them for dying in the first place." At funerals, when we say things like, "He would have liked it this way," we keep his characteristics fresh in our minds by speaking in an ambiguous past/present tense. Writing about the same phenomenon, the philosopher Daniel Dennett notes that people in bereavement cannot stop thinking of their loved ones as *intentional agents* and *mindful personalities*.[38] I conclude that a mourner exhibits a tacit dualist philosophy when he or she acts as though the mind of the loved one has survived the death of the body.

Children, too, have a notion of life after death, indicating that the concept is not the product of education or indoctrination. Jesse Bering and David Bjorkland arranged for children to attend a puppet show featuring an animated Mr. Alligator who eats an animated Brown Mouse.[39] After the children had seen the video, the investigators interviewed the kids to learn what they thought was extinguished when the mouse died and what, if anything, survived. They asked three types of questions. A typical *biological* question was, "Now that Brown Mouse is not alive anymore, do you think that he will ever need to drink water again?" *Psychobiological* questions were of the sort, "Now that the mouse is no longer alive, is he still hungry?" The remaining questions probed *cognitive* functions, for example, "Now that the mouse is no longer alive, does he know that he's not alive?" Already at ages 4–6 years, 78 percent of the children understood that biological functions do not survive after death. Interestingly, however, 67 percent of the children believed that psychological functions *do* survive after death, and 62 percent believed that cognitive functions survive after death. These findings indicate that very young children think that psychological and mental functions continue even after the body has ceased to function. The authors conclude that "these beliefs [in an afterlife] are characterized by a highly typical complexion: that of a knowing, believing, *mindful* spirit that has shed its biology proper [emphasis in the original]."[40]

Table 3.1   Results from a Gallup poll on American beliefs in paranormal phenomena

Belief	Percent believing
Extrasensory perception	41
Houses can be haunted	37
Ghosts (spirits of dead people can come back)	32
Telepathy (direct communication between minds)	31
Clairvoyance (the power of the mind to know the past and predict the future)	26
Astrology (the position of the stars and planets can affect people's lives)	25
People can communicate mentally with someone who has died	21
Witches	21
Reincarnation (the rebirth of the soul in a new body after death)	20
Channeling (allowing a 'spirit-being' to temporarily assume control of one's body)	9

It might be argued that the idea of an immaterial, unknowable mind-stuff controlling activity in the brain is simply too outlandish for anyone to believe. The polls show, however, that people actually believe in many things that are at least as bizarre as the mind substance, stuff that has absolutely no basis in modern science. Take, for example, a 2005 Gallup poll that tallied Americans' beliefs in certain paranormal phenomena. Gallup defined the paranormal as any phenomenon that requires the use of "more than the 'normal' five senses."[41]

Remarkably, Gallup's analysis revealed that 73 percent of the respondents believed in at least one of the queried items (Table 3.1). It is noteworthy, too, that most of the listed items refer to either imagined powers of the mind (telepathy, clairvoyance, and reincarnation) or supernatural beings (ghosts, witches, and channeling). Taken together, the data strongly suggest that the absence of material evidence is no barrier to belief. Given a sufficiently compelling subjective experience, people will believe in just about anything. I am arguing that the experience of consciousness is enough to convince most people that dualism is real.

A Critique of Descartes' Dualism

Critics claim that philosophy is painfully slow in resolving anything that really matters. It is true that important issues remain unresolved, at least in the philosophy of mind, but it would be mistaken to say that there has been no progress. Of particular interest to us is the history of criticism of Descartes' mind–body philosophy. As the discussion below will demonstrate, there are good reasons for rejecting Descartes' arguments on logical and empirical grounds. Later, in chapter 5, I will examine some of the many ideas that have been proposed as alternatives to Descartes' dualism.

We begin with Descartes' famous *Cogito* statement and its related passages, which I quoted above. Descartes says, "I think, therefore I am." From this he concludes that he is "a substance whose whole essence or nature is only that of thinking." He goes on to state that his soul (or mind) exists and that it is distinct from his body. There are a couple of serious problems with these assertions.[42] First, it is plainly illogical to go from a statement that one cannot think without existing, to the claim that one's whole essence is to think. Second, just because he says that he is certain about these things, it does not mean that they are true. Descartes himself described how he was sometimes deluded by dreams. Nevertheless, in his book, *Meditations on First Philosophy*, he presented what he thought was the ultimate argument for the reliability of intuitions. God, he said, would not allow something to be untrue if it were perceived "clearly and distinctly." Descartes felt secure in claiming that the soul exists independently of the body because he himself perceived it clearly and distinctly, but intuition alone is a weak foundation for metaphysics. We can also note the circularity of Descartes' clear and distinct argument. While he relies on God for the truthfulness of intuitions that are clear and distinct, his proof of the existence of God is itself based on clear and distinct intuitions.

Another problem in Cartesian dualism is its account of the interactions between mind and brain. You will recall that he identified the pineal gland as the presumed site of interaction. Descartes' error lies not in his choice of location—even if we ridicule it today—but in the absence of any credible suggestion as to *how* the interactions could occur. Despite his keen interest in mechanics, nowhere in any of his published works does Descartes attempt to explain how mind can affect brain, or vice versa. Even in his lifetime, several of Descartes' contemporaries found this odd. For example, his friend and frequent correspondent, the Princess Elizabeth of Bohemia, badgered him to explain, but he did not.

Just think for a moment about the two postulated substances, mind and brain. Imagine again that you decide to move your hand. In order for this to happen, certain neurons in your precentral gyrus must fire action potentials. Because action potentials require the flow of electrical charges across the cell membrane, there can be no movement of the hand unless tiny channels first open in the membrane. To open the channels, parts of certain proteins must momentarily shift their positions. Does the mind stuff open the channels? How, exactly, could this work? We can describe the process in biophysical terms because we know a lot about molecules and their interactions, but nothing that we know about mind can explain how it could open channels in nerve cell membranes. No philosopher, nor any scientist, has provided a plausible hypothesis. Not even John C. Eccles, one of the greatest neuroscientists of the twentieth century and an ardent defender of Cartesian dualism, could come up with a coherent hypothesis for how the mind might cause things to happen in the brain.[43] On the contrary, physicists point to the law of the conservation of energy, which states that energy is neither gained nor lost in a closed or isolated system.

Since Descartes describes mind as distinct and separate from the brain, hence isolated, an interaction between the two would necessarily require a flow of energy from the mind to the brain and then back the other way, and that would violate the principle of conservation.

Gilbert Ryle, an influential British philosopher of the mid-twentieth century, offered a very different criticism of Descartes. He described Descartes' concept of the mind as "the doctrine of the ghost in the machine" and "a philosopher's myth." In his book, *The Concept of Mind*,[44] Ryle argues that the whole idea of interaction between the mind and the brain is false because it is based on a logical error known as the *category mistake*. Logic dictates that interactions should occur only when the interacting "things" belong to the same category, for example, when a billiard cue strikes a billiard ball; in this example, both elements in the interaction are *physical objects*. However, no interaction is possible between the ball and the *name* of the game, billiards, because in this case, one thing is a physical object and the other thing is a name. Descartes assumed that interaction is possible because both the mind and the brain are both *substances.* In fact, says Ryle, the brain is a substance, but the mind is nothing but an inference that people draw from their observations of behavior. Therefore, the mind and the brain are fundamentally different, they belong to different categories of things, and interaction is inconceivable.

In addition to the philosophical arguments, there is also empirical evidence contradicting one of Descartes' major claims, namely, that the mind "needs no other thing in order to exist." Is it possible that he did know about traumatic brain injuries? Accidents involving the brain can create mental confusion and induce comatose states. When these changes of subjective state occur one also sees unmistakable signs of altered electrical activity in the brain. Sometimes a physician will intentionally induce a coma in order to stabilize the patient; in these cases too, brain activity subsides. More telling still, in cases of induced comas, consciousness can be quickly restored by carrying out certain physical procedures prescribed by the doctor. The mind's dependence on the brain is also shown by the effectiveness of "mind-altering" drugs such as antidepressants, hallucinogens, and alcohol.

Mental activity can be altered in a dramatic fashion by electrical stimulation of the brain. Wilder Penfield demonstrated this in a series of famous experiments performed on patients who were undergoing brain surgeries.[45] As part of the procedure for determining the precise area of the brain that had to be removed, Penfield inserted a fine metal electrode and passed a small electrical current into the brain. The patients were awake and cooperative during the tests. At certain locations, the current elicited vivid subjective experiences, described by the patients as detailed reenactments of memories. One patient heard a favorite song and another described the view from her childhood window. In a similar recent case, electrical stimulation in the brain of a young woman caused her to laugh and feel merry.[46] Also, transcranial electrical stimulation (TES) and transcranial magnetic stimulation (TMS) are said to be effective tools for controlling moods. What is important in all these examples is not simply the *correlation* of brain events and mind events, but rather the *causal dependence* of mind states on brain states.

The arguments that I have summarized above will be familiar to most students of philosophy. They have been expressed, in one form or another, by many of the eminent philosophers of the past including Thomas Hobbes, John Locke, Gottfried Wilhelm Leibniz, Immanuel Kant, and Bertrand Russell. Likewise, a clear majority of contemporary philosophers and neuroscientists rejects Cartesian dualism,[47] although there are exceptions.[48] One of the most outspoken critics of René Descartes is Daniel Dennett of Tufts University. In his best-selling book, *Consciousness Explained*, Dennett calls dualism "forlorn" and says that Descartes' notion of the mind "wallows in mystery."[49] In the following passage, Dennett suggests an interesting explanation for why certain of his philosophical colleagues are undeterred by dualism's obvious shortcomings.

> It is surely no accident that the few dualists to avow their views openly have all candidly and comfortably announced that they have no theory whatever of how the mind works—something, they insist, that is quite beyond human ken. There is the lurking suspicion that the most attractive feature of the mind stuff is its promise of being *so* mysterious that it keeps science at bay forever.[50]

Evolutionary Considerations

Descartes wrote that mind exists only in humans and that animals are mere machines. He assumed that humans became intentional, conscious agents through divine intervention, while animals were left to operate as pure neuromuscular actors. But who can say whether a dog thinks or a worm feels? If your golden retriever whimpers as you put on your coat, perhaps it does enjoy a moment of joyful anticipation. Scientists are increasingly willing to conclude that dogs, chimpanzees, crows, and other species have cognitive abilities and intentional behaviors.[51] Few people doubt, however, that humans are the most conscious of all animals. Therefore, while Descartes may have ascribed mind to humans alone because he wished to place humans on a "higher" plane, he might just as well have distributed mind throughout the animal kingdom in proportion to inferences drawn from their overt behaviors. Man would still have come out on top.

If we assume, contrary to Descartes, that some animals have at least some degree of consciousness and some use of intentional mental states, then how this came to be the case becomes a matter of speculative interest. It is possible, of course, to invoke creationism and to declare that God placed just the right amount of mind in each of his gifts. However, most educated people, including many dualists, will reject this scenario in favor of an explanation based in science. According to evolutionary (Darwinian) theory, traits appear and become modified through the differential propagation of genetic variants, or DNA mutations. DNA makes RNA, which makes proteins, which build the body and the brain. In other words, evolution has a physical basis. Therefore, a hypothetical scenario for the evolution of mind must involve incremental changes in the nervous system. Nerve cells have the same basic properties—structural, chemical, and physiological—in all animals, but genetic variation causes the *number* of neurons and the *organization* of the nervous system to differ greatly in different species, thus allowing consciousness and intentionality to emerge progressively as the brain becomes increasingly complex. This, at least, is a plausible explanation for the evolution of mind. By contrast, on the view that the mind is entirely separate from the brain and has no physicality, the entire Darwinian theory is irrelevant and there is no way to explain the appearance of mind in either animals or humans except by divine intervention.

In speculating on the evolution of mind, it is appropriate to focus on consciousness, not only because it is integral to any concept of mind, but also because there could have been no philosophy of dualism without consciousness. Not until early man began to reflect on his conscious self could he have imagined such a thing as mind. Indeed, it is clear from Descartes' statements, notably the *Cogito*, that Descartes' fascination with his own consciousness engendered Cartesian dualism. Thus, it is reasonable to ask when consciousness first appeared in humans, and under what circumstances.

The first anatomically modern humans, *Homo sapiens*, date to about 200,000 years ago. We were probably social creatures from the very beginning, and many commentators have suggested that human consciousness evolved together with language as a response to our growing social activities. An early advocate of this view was Friedrich Nietzsche, who wrote in 1887,

> As the most endangered animal, he [humans] *needed* help and pro-
> tection, he needed his peers, he had to learn to express his distress
> and to make himself understood; and for all of this he needed "con-
> sciousness" first of all, he needed to "know" himself what distressed
> him, he needed to "know" how he felt, he needed to "know" what he
> thought. For, to say it once more: Man, like every living being, thinks
> continually without knowing it; the thinking that rises *consciousness*
> is only the smallest part of all this—the most superficial and worst
> part—for only this conscious thinking *takes the form of words, which
> is to say signs of communications*, and this fact uncovers the origin
> of consciousness.[52]

Scientific evidence suggests that language evolved relatively recently in our evolutionary past. It is thought that an early first step was the downward movement of the larynx, because the high position of the larynx in modern apes does not allow for controlled and articulated vocalizations. Changes in brain anatomy must also have occurred, and the gene FOXP2 is implicated as an agent in these adaptations. Evidence for the involvement of FOXP2 came initially from the discovery of mutations in the gene in several members of an extended family, all of whom suffer from speech deficits.[53] FOXP2 is known to have a role in early brain development, especially in regions that have language functions, inviting some scientists to propose that a beneficial mutation in this gene was the key that opened the door for human language. Geneticists estimate that the mutation occurred between 100,000 and 10,000 years ago. Assuming that language arose at one time and in one place, and given that *Homo sapiens* migrated out of Africa to colonize the rest of the planet about 75,000 years ago, a reasonable estimate for the emergence of human language would be 75,000–100,000 years ago. If consciousness did indeed evolve together with language, it would have first appeared at about the same time.

Other commentators have proposed different scenarios. The neuro-scientist Christof Koch, for example, thinks that consciousness evolved not as an adjunct to social communication but as a tool used by the brain to evaluate situations requiring plans for actions.[54] Nicholas Humphrey, an experimental psychologist and an astute philosopher of mind, believes that consciousness evolved to create a sense of self, which then functions as a motivator in human lives.

> Consciousness matters *because it is its function to matter.* It has been designed to create in human beings a Self whose life is worth pursuing . . . . My suggestion is that in the course of human evolution, our ancestors who thought of their own consciousness as metaphysically remarkable—existing outside normal space and time—would have taken themselves still more seriously as Selves. The more mysterious and unworldly the qualities of consciousness, the more seriously significant the Self. And the more significant the Self, the greater the boost to human self-confidence and self-importance—and the greater the value that individuals place on their own and others' lives.[55]

One intrepid scholar claims that consciousness originated very recently. In his extraordinary book, *The Origin of Consciousness in the Breakdown of the Bicameral Mind,* Julian Jaynes lays out an unorthodox history based on written texts.[56] He claims that the earliest artifacts—chiseled stones dating from the second and third millennia BC—reflect a time when people had no sense of self and no consciousness.[57] Human behavior, he states, was governed by automatisms and the voices of gods. To explain this, he imagines that people long ago had *bicameral,* or two-chambered, minds. What these people actually experienced when they "heard" the commands of gods were auditory hallucinations originating in the right temporal lobe of the cerebral cortex. The left hemisphere of the cerebral cortex received these messages and carried out the commands.

Jaynes also relies on a linguistic analysis of the *Iliad* to build his case. Although often attributed to one man, Homer, the stories in the *Iliad* were probably written down over a long period of time, roughly between the years 1,230 BC and 850 BC. Jaynes believes that even at this late date the Mycenaeans were still bicameral men lacking consciousness. Two short examples give a sense of his argument.

> The words in the Iliad that in a later age come to mean mental things have different meanings, all of them more concrete. The word *psyche,* which later means soul or conscious mind, is in most instances life-substances, such as blood or breath: a dying warrior bleeds out his *psyche* onto the ground or breathes it out in his last gasp.[58]

> Perhaps most important is the word *noos* which, spelled as *nous* in later Greek, comes to mean conscious mind. It comes from the *noeein*, to see. Its proper translation in the Iliad would be something like perception or recognition or field of vision. Zeus "holds Odysseus in his *noos*." He keeps watch over him.[59]

Eventually, according to Jaynes, several factors contributed to the breakdown of the bicameral mind, among which were "the weakening of the auditory by the advent of writing," "the unworkableness of gods in the chaos of historical upheaval," and "a modicum of natural selection." As the bicameral mind gradually disappeared and consciousness took its place, human mentality changed fundamentally. In Greece, writes Jaynes, these changes happened relatively recently, even as late as the first millennium BC. Overall, Jaynes gives us an intriguing argument that cannot be lightly dismissed, but the evidence falls short of proof.

Summary and Forward Glance

Réne Descartes took an old idea, fancied it up, and presented it in a language that ordinary people could readily understand. Nearly five centuries later, I think that most people today accept his concept of the mind as valid and true. We cannot be sure of this, however, because there have been no credible opinion polls. Also, dualism survives more as a tacit assumption than as an explicit philosophy of mind. Nevertheless, one can find indirect evidence for the influence of dualism in our intuitions, our language, our religions, and even in our entertainments. Despite its popularity, dualism is a flawed philosophy of mind. It is supported largely by intuition and weak arguments, while contradicted by neurological experiments.

People are not stupid for believing in dualism. Rather, dualism is a consequence of our biological evolution. Our brains evolved to meet certain challenges, among which was the human social environment, and part of what came out of that process was a brain that generates consciousness. Dualism is a by-product of consciousness; Descartes himself formulated his philosophy of mind only after contemplating his consciousness. However, just because Descartes, or anyone else, believes in an immaterial mind does not mean that such a thing exists.

A situation analogous to dualistic philosophy applies to the way in which our brains perceive the physical environment. As Richard Dawkins explains in his brilliant concept of the *middle world*,[60] our senses evolved primarily to function in the recognition of objects of potential benefit or harm. We perceive objects according to our needs, not as they really are. Rocks, for example, are composed of molecules, which are themselves composed of atoms. Within each atom is a nucleus surrounded by electrons, and in between these tiny particles is a vast amount of space. So, while physics tells us that rocks are mostly empty, we perceive them as solids. The reason why we maintain such false beliefs about rocks, walls, and other seemingly solid objects is because we need to know that rocks are heavy and walls cannot be walked through. Whereas people who have not had the benefit of an education in physics know nothing of the vast spaces within rocks and walls, people who do know about the spaces understandably *ignore them in their everyday lives*. Similarly, few people are familiar with the arguments against dualism, and those who do know the arguments *ignore them in their everyday lives*. Just as our evolutionary history biases us to believe in solid objects, so too does it bias us to believe in gods, to use folk psychology, and to view ourselves as something besides mere bodies.

The mind is commonly associated with intentions, beliefs, feelings, and the like. These are the very things that become disturbed in the major mental illnesses. So, if the mind were a real thing, it would be reasonable to speak of an illness *in the mind*, a dysfunctional condition affecting that thing, the mind. Irrational or troublesome behavior would be explained as the product of a sick mind influencing an otherwise healthy brain. On the other hand, if it is the case, as I believe it to be, that Descartes' dualism is erroneous and that there is no substantive mind, then we need a different account of mental illness. A further motive for discarding dualism is that it fosters ideas that are detrimental to the welfare of persons living with mental illness, as we will learn in the next chapter.

Notes

1. Word frequency counts are from Leech et al., 2001. For summaries, see http://ucrel.lancs.ac.uk/bncfreq/.
2. Reported by Wilford, 2008.
3. Russell, 1945.
4. I have translated Anaxagoras's word *nous*, as *mind*, but it can also be translated as *soul*. The ancient Greeks also used the word, *psuche* or *psyche*, which likewise has the meanings *mind* and *soul*, depending on context and interpretation. My practice will be to insert the English word that best matches the author's conception when quoting or discussing a specific author. Thus, *mind* for Anaxagoras, *soul* for Plato.

5. http://classics.mit.edu/Plato/phaedo.html.
6. For an analysis of Aristotle's writings on the soul, see Flew, 1971, pp. 159–67.
7. Quoted in Flew, 1971, p. 165.
8. Descartes, 1637, Part IV. See Descartes, 1965.
9. Descartes, 1637, Part IV. See Descartes, 1965.
10. Descartes, 1644, Part one, principles LI and LII. See Descartes, 1965.
11. Robinson, H., Dualism, *The Stanford Encyclopedia of Philosophy* (Winter 2007), E.N. Zalta (ed.), http://plato.stanford.edu/archives/win2007/entries/dualism/.
12. Descartes, *The Passions of the Soul*, 1650, article XXX. See Descartes, 1965.
13. Descartes, 1637, Part V. See Descartes, 1965.
14. For a complete account of Descartes' pineal hypothesis, see Lokhorst, G.-J., Descartes and the pineal gland, *The Stanford Encyclopedia of Philosophy* (Spring 2009), E.N. Zalta (ed.), http://plato.stanford.edu/archives/spr2009/entries/pineal-gland/.
15. To be described in chapter 5.
16. Embree and Embree, 1993.
17. Boyer, 2001.
18. Ravenscroft, I., Folk psychology as a theory, *The Stanford Encyclopedia of Philosophy* (Fall 2008), E.N. Zalta (ed.), http://plato.stanford.edu/archives/fall2008/entries/folkpsych-theory/.
19. Baron-Cohen, 1995.
20. Popper and Eccles, 1977.
21. Heider and Simmel, 1944.
22. Bloom, 2004a.
23. Estes et al., 1998.
24. Bloom, 2004b.
25. Interview with Natasha Mitchell on Australian radio, http://www.abc.net.au/rn/allinthemind/stories/2008/2276587.htm.
26. Bloom, 2004b.
27. Bloom, 2004a, p. 186.
28. Schomerus et al., 2008.
29. Gallup poll, http://www.gallup.com/poll/109108/Belief-God-Far-Lower-Western-US.aspx.
30. Pew Forum on Religion and Public Life, http://religions.pewforum.org/?sid=ST2008062300818.
31. Barrett and Keil, 1996.
32. Stated in the Lankaventara Sutra.
33. Nicosia, 1994.
34. CBS poll, http://www.cbsnews.com/stories/2005/10/29/opinion/polls/main994766.shtml. Gallup poll, http://www.gallup.com/poll/17275/One-Third-Americans-Believe-Dearly-May-Departed.aspx.
35. Boyer, 2001, p. 227.
36. Greeley and Hout, 1999.
37. Boyer, 2001.
38. Dennett, 2007.
39. Bering and Bjorkland, 2004.

40. Ibid., p. 230.
41. Gallup poll, http://www.gallup.com/poll/16915/Three-Four-Americans-Believe-Paranormal.aspx.
42. For the full arguments, see Williams, 1978.
43. Popper and Eccles, 1977.
44. Ryle, 1949.
45. Penfield, 1958.
46. Fried et al., 1998.
47. Examples include philosophers, Churchland, 1986; Dennett, 1991; neuro-scientists, Crick, 1994; Damasio, 2005.
48. Examples include philosophers, Hart, 1988; Foster, 1991; neuroscientists, Penfield, 1975; Beauregard and O'Leary, 2007.
49. Dennett, 1991.
50. Ibid., p. 37.
51. Shettleworth, 2010.
52. Nietzsche, 1887, pp. 298–99.
53. Enard et al., 2002.
54. Koch, 2004.
55. Humphrey, 2006, pp. 131–32.
56. Jaynes, 1982.
57. Interestingly, Jaynes does not mention the Egyptian *Book of the Dead* (ca. 1,500 BC), which arguably contains evidence of dualistic thinking; see p. 27.
58. Ibid., p. 69.
59. Ibid., p. 70
60. http://www.ted.com/index.php/talks/richard_dawkins_on_our_queer_universe.html.Table 3.1 Results from a Gallup poll on American beliefs in paranormal phenomena

4

Dualism Supports Stigmatization and Other Unhelpful Attitudes

Dualism, an idea of pure metaphysics, not only enters into our intellectual understanding of mental illness, but it also influences our actions in respect to affected individuals. In this chapter, I will explain how dualistic assumptions shape attitudes that discriminate against persons with mental illnesses and negatively affect their treatments. Dualism has these effects because it posits a mind that is independent and free. Freedom of the will can be seen to imply, at least in the minds of dualists, that one is free to become insane.

Ordinarily, and appropriately, we hold people responsible for their actions, but there are circumstances in which attributions of responsibility are wrongheaded, and mental illness is one of them. When we insist upon holding the mentally ill responsible for their own illnesses, we ignore the true biological causes, and bad consequences follow.

The idea that mental disturbances are voluntary dates from the nineteenth century. Previous to that time, bizarre behaviors were attributed to forces outside of the individual, be they gods or demons. Following upon the new modes of thinking that characterized the Enlightenment in the eighteenth century, significant changes occurred in the European asylums for the insane. Noteworthy here are the reforms initiated by William Tuke and Philippe Pinel. Tuke had an asylum at York, England, under the auspices of the local Quaker community, while Pinel headed two large, publicly funded asylums near Paris, one for women at Bicêtre and another for men at Salpêtrière. Their reforms included improvements to physical conditions, the elimination of inhumane practices, and earnest attempts to find effective treatments. Most importantly, both Tuke and Pinel created programs of rehabilitation which came to be known as *moral therapies*.[1] The goal of moral therapy was to make patients behave in a manner conforming to social and religious norms. The treatment regime, which occasionally involved physical punishments, was designed to make the patients recognize and correct their own abnormal behaviors. The tasks of the caretakers were firstly, to convince the patients that they themselves were responsible for their behaviors, and secondly, to motivate them to behave normally. Underlying the procedures was the philosophical assumption of an unbounded human spirit, one always capable of personal betterment. One historian has referred to the attitude as a "starry-eyed conviction in the power of the will."[2]

When an ill person exhibits physical signs of pathology, almost everyone will recognize the illness as involuntary. However, the interpretation is less obvious when there is no physical evidence, as was the case with mental illness in the nineteenth century. The moral therapists decided that the illnesses were voluntary, and they designed their treatment programs accordingly. Today, we have many biological markers of mental illness, among which are altered brain structures, mutated genes, and abnormal neurochemistry.[3] Nevertheless, I believe that the notion of voluntary mental illness persists today and that it is a significant factor in causing stigma, for reasons that I explain below.

Stigmatization

When men living in ancient Greece were tattooed, they were said to receive a *stigma*, or mark. Today, the stigma of mental illness is not visible, but nonetheless highly consequential. The word itself has been redefined to signify the identification of a person with undesirable characteristics. Mental illness stigmata are prevalent and damaging, as evidenced by recent surveys. In one American survey, for example, only 46 percent of respondents said that they would tell friends if they had been treated for schizophrenia.[4] Similarly, only 50 percent of respondents in a 2008 survey conducted for the Canadian Medical Association said that they would tell friends or coworkers that they have a family member suffering from mental illness, compared to 72 percent for diagnoses of cancer and 68 percent for diabetes.[5] The same survey found that 46 percent of Canadians agree with the statement, "We call some things mental illness because it gives some people an excuse for their poor behavior and personal failings." Commenting upon these numbers, the president of the Canadian Medical Association,

Dr. Brian Day, observed that "[w]e are looking at the final frontier of socially acceptable discrimination."

Nor are professional caretakers immune to negative stereotyping. Swiss investigators interviewed more than one thousand mental health professionals at twenty-nine German-speaking hospitals.[6] Their responses to a questionnaire were compared with those obtained from a random sample of the Swiss population, and a quantitative measure of stereotypic attitude was determined for each respondent. The results showed that, overall, the professionals and the general population held equally negative views of the mentally ill. Even more remarkably, a statistical comparison among the several groups of professionals revealed that the psychiatrists' attitudes were significantly more negative than those of every other professional type (psychologists, nurses, and other therapists). In the authors' words, "The study concludes that the better knowledge of mental health professionals and their support of individual rights neither entail fewer stereotypes nor enhance the willingness to closely interact with mentally ill people."

Stigma acts in many ways to disadvantage persons with mental illness. It blocks employment, ends friendships, disrupts spousal relationships, and frustrates virtually all life goals that are dependent on social interactions. Stigmatization also seems to affect how well people are able to overcome their mental illnesses. Some studies indicate that the prognosis for mental illness is better in societies with little stigmatization than in societies with intense stigmatization; the difference seems to lie in the degree of sympathy and social support.[7] Furthermore, stigma probably keeps many individuals from seeking professional help for their mental illnesses. In the Canadian study mentioned above, persons who had experienced three or more signs of mental illness in the previous year were asked how they dealt with their problems. Twenty percent of the respondents said that they dealt with them either on their own or by ignoring them—this, despite the availability of Canada's publicly-funded health care system. Studies in the United States estimate that "nearly two-thirds of all people with diagnosable mental disorders do not seek treatment."[8] Not everyone who foregoes treatment does so because of the associated stigma, but even if stigma accounts for only a fraction of these people, the elimination of stigma would still yield significant cost savings from increased productivity and greater self-sufficiency. This was the conclusion, anyway, of the Global Business and Economic Roundtable on

Addiction and Mental Health as reported in Canadian newspapers under the headline, "Employers could save billions by reducing stigma of mental illness."[9]

There are two sides to stigma. On one side are the attitudes of the healthy in respect to the ill, while on the other side are the attitudes of the mentally ill persons in respect to themselves. In the latter case, the internalized stigma creates shame and *self-stigma*. Here is how one individual describes her experience of self-stigma:

> While we all know that stigmatization of the mentally ill exists and that it is always harmful, there is a kind of stigma that is actually more damaging than that inflicted by others. It is the all-too-real process and phenomenon of "self-stigmatization" whereby mentally ill individuals torture themselves to an extent that exceeds what they suffer from the very worst that society-at-large can dish out to them . . . . When I first joined [a rehabilitation facility], I was in hiding from everyone. I perceived myself, quite accurately, unfortunately, as having a serious mental illness and therefore as having been relegated to what I called "the social garbage heap."[10]

Thankfully, the author of the preceding passage succeeded in regaining her self-esteem. Others, less fortunate, suffer not only the cognitive impairments of the illness but also the shame that goes with it. Interestingly, Francis Broucek, an authority on shame, says that a person feels shame when his or her personal identity has been damaged. Moreover, in his book, *Shame and the Self*, Broucek argues that it is impossible to experience shame unless one adopts a dualistic attitude toward the mind, because dualism makes it possible for the shamed person to reflect on his or her self.[11]

The Sources of Stigma: Irrational Violence

The pernicious effects of mental illness stigma invite efforts to understand its origins, for only then can it be effectively combated.[12] There is a pressing need for this because the high levels of stigma that have been apparent for decades show little or no sign of decline.[13] The causes of stigma are controversial, and no doubt multiple, but I believe that a number of factors explain stigma, including the fear of irrational violence, moral judgments, and attributions of responsibility. Entering into each of these putative causes are assumptions related to the Cartesian mind.

Public opinion surveys consistently find that people associate mental illness with violence.[14] The news media and the entertainment industry are largely responsible for sustaining this stereotype because they exploit certain sensational examples for their own purposes. In reality, persons with mental illness are only slightly more prone to violence than the general population.[15] Furthermore, epidemiological studies find that the risk of violence is limited, almost entirely, to cases in which a severe mental illness is combined with either drug abuse or drug dependency. The known facts are put in perspective by Eric Elbogen and Sally Johnson, commenting on the results of their study.

> Such data [their own] are at odds with public fears such as those reported in a national survey in which 75% of the sample viewed people with mental illness as dangerous and 60% believed people with schizophrenia were likely to commit violent acts. Instead, the current results show that if a person has severe mental illness without substance abuse and history of violence, he or she has the same chances of being violent during the next 3 years as any other person in the general population.[16]

Some surveys ask people separate questions about their fear of violence and their readiness, or lack thereof, to form social relationships with persons described as mentally ill. Answers to the latter set of questions yield the so-called *social distance measure*, which is a measure of stigma. In a frequently cited study authored by Bruce Link and colleagues,[17] each participant was presented with a single vignette from a battery of five possible vignettes; four of the vignettes described "psychiatric disorders" (alcohol dependency, major depression, schizophrenia, cocaine dependency), while the fifth described a "troubled person." After listening to the vignette, the participant was asked a set of questions to determine his or her sense of social distance from the person described in the vignette. The data showed that there is "an appreciable association between the belief that a person is likely to be violent and the desire to maintain social distance from that person." One might mistakenly conclude from this result that the fear of violence *causes* the desire for social distance, but the authors themselves carefully avoid this conclusion. What the data actually show is a statistical *correlation*, meaning that, on average, people who felt that the person in the vignette would be violent *also* wished to keep a social distance from that person. Note that violence and stigma are not always correlated; for example, we may fear the violence of policemen and soldiers, yet we stigmatize neither group.

In my opinion, people do not so much fear violence in the mentally ill as they fear irrationality and unpredictability. Negative attitudes toward irrationality are commonplace, as expressed by Plato among others. When rationality fails, behavior becomes unpredictable (by the theory of mind), and violence is seen as a possible, but uncertain, outcome. While we may expect violence from the police and from soldiers, it is the less predictable violence of mental patients that creates the greater fear. The idea of irrationality was central to Michel Foucault's celebrated interpretation of madness in the eighteenth century.[18] It was the fear of irrationality, he wrote, that drove people to treat the mentally ill so harshly. The equally distinguished English historian, Roy Porter, took strong issue with Foucault on some matters—such as the true extent of punishing treatments—but he endorsed Foucault's "particularly valuable" insight that the key characteristic attributed to mentally ill persons in the eighteenth century was irrationality. Porter said of Foucault that,

> what he was writing—indeed, what must be written—was a history of reason or rationality, as a necessary condition for a history of madness or irrationality. History cannot understand the constitution of madness without first understanding what constituted it as madness—without, in other words, accepting how the progress of the subject, Reason, presupposes its own negation.[19]

Schizophrenia is stigmatized more than any other mental illness, perhaps due to the symptom of disorderly or irrational thought. It is interesting to note, therefore, that another contributing factor is the conception of schizophrenia as an illness *in the mind*. The observations of Yoshiharu Kim and Qerman Berrios support this statement.[20] These psychiatrists compared how schizophrenia is viewed in Asian versus Western societies. Their interesting conclusion is that schizophrenia is more stigmatized in Asian countries than in English speaking countries because of differences in the writing systems. The English word *schizophrenia* comes from two Greek words meaning "splitting of mental faculties." Kim and Berrios believe that the literal meaning of the word has been lost to most Westerners, notwithstanding its occasional misapplication. Asians use a writing system based on ideographs, and the ideographic equivalent of *schizophrenia* prior to 2002 contained five characters that combine to create three independent terms: *Seishin-Bunretsu-Byo*. The translation is exactly "mind-split-disease." Each of the three component terms is common in the Japanese language, and each has an unambiguous meaning. Therefore, the meaning of *schizophrenia* in its ideographic construction before 2002 was automatically understood as "the disease of disordered mind." [21] According to Kim and Berrios, "The term directly challenges a deeply ingrained concept of *personal autonomy*, and this is stigmatizing [italics added]." It would be fair to say that the authors' reference to personal autonomy evokes the closely related concept of rational free will. In 2002, a new term for schizophrenia was officially adopted, *Togo-Shitcho-Sho*, literally meaning "integration disorder." Interestingly, the change of name seems to have reduced stigma.[22]

In a different way, the link between stigma, irrationality, and mind is also evident in this comment written by Shirley Star, one of the pioneer researchers in the field of mental illness stigma.

> Mental illness is a very threatening, fearful thing and not an idea to be entertained lightly about anyone. Emotionally, it represents to people a loss of what they consider to be the distinctively human qualities of rationality and free will, and there is a kind of a horror in dehumanization. As both our data and other studies make clear, mental illness is something that people want to keep as far from themselves as possible.[23]

If thinking is in the mind, as Descartes proposed, then irrational thinking is also in the mind. Moreover, Descartes insisted that the mind is completely free to initiate actions, giving rise to the notion of free will. From these premises flows the notion that individuals are personally responsible for their illnesses, and this supposition is an important element in the process of stigmatization, as we will see in the next section. Evidently, the office of the United States Surgeon General agrees with this line of argument because, in its 1999 Report on Mental Health, it stated (without elaboration), "Explanations for stigma stem, in part, from the misguided split between mind and body first proposed by Descartes."[24]

The Sources of Stigma: Attributions of Personal Responsibility

In Western societies, we tend to think that physical illnesses, at least, are caused by physical events such as infections, gene mutations, and organ failures. Elsewhere, however, other types of explanations prevail. Richard Shweder and his anthropological colleagues studied how people in different regions of the world react to suffering.[25] Their findings led them to write,

[I]t is helpful to keep in mind the true aims of causal analysis in folk psychology: to set abnormal outcomes right by gaining control over abnormal conditions that are within the range of one's expertise and power, and to attribute responsibility and to assign fault in a world of events presumed to be caused by "free and deliberate" acts by "conscious and responsible" agents.[26]

Shweder *et al.* specifically address the explanations for mental illnesses. Their important finding is that,

when it comes to explaining afflictions such as insanity or death, the folk around the world almost never concern themselves with biomedical causes and almost always explain it in either other-blaming interpersonal terms or agent-blaming moral terms.[27]

The statements quoted above strongly suggest that moral concerns underlie the most common reactions to mental illness. Shweder *et al.* further describe the two main types of explanation. In traditional societies, the *interpersonal causal explanation* relates to sorcery, evil eye, black magic, spirit attack, poisoning, and bewitchment, whereas in developed societies it relates to harassment, abuse, exploitation, codependencies, and toxic relationships. The *moral causal explanation* has the same connotation in both traditional and developed societies, namely, "omissions of duty, trespass of mandatory boundaries, and more generally any type of ethical failure at decision making or self-control. It is associated with the idea that suffering is the result of one's own actions or intentions."[28]

Although Shweder *et al.* conducted their field work among traditional societies in South Asia, they contend that the findings can be applied more broadly. Regarding mental illness in particular, they voice the opinion that moral and interpersonal explanations of mental illness are not limited to South Asia, or even to traditional cultures. On the contrary, these types of explanation are common everywhere, but typically suppressed and disguised. Even in the United States, say Shweder *et al.*, these ideas

persist as "private" intuitions experienced as mysteries or with embarrassment or as personal or communal "counter-discourses" to the official discourse of scientific explanation . . . . It is our assumption that ideas about human experience that persist long, or are widespread, or become invested with social meaning and established as folk theories in a major region of the world are not likely to be merely "primitive" or "superstitious." It is our assumption that such ideas illuminate some aspect of mind, experience, or society.[29]

We can draw two conclusions from the studies of Shweder *et al.* First, not only are biomedical explanations of mental illness shunned by "folk around the world," but psychological explanations—Freudian or otherwise—are also generally ignored. Second, the favored explanations—interpersonal and moral—are those for which personal responsibility can be, and is, assigned. Mental illness is caused either by one's own moral transgressions or by another person's transgressions. Some *one* is responsible. Given that blaming the victim is a major contributing factor to stigma, it will be useful to examine the psychological and philosophical contexts for judgments of blame. Central to these concerns is the concept of free will.

Descartes looked upon animals as nothing but complex machines, or famously, *bêtes machines.* He said that the human body is also a machine, but in addition and uniquely, humans have minds (= souls). He further believed that a key property of the human mind is its power to make decisions and initiate actions. In other words, free will is a property of the mind. Descartes wrote in his *Meditations,*

> It is free will alone or liberty of choice which I find to be so great in me that I can conceive no other idea to be more great; it is indeed the case that it is for the most part this will that causes me to know that in some manner I bear the image and similitude of God. For although the power of will is incomparably greater in God than in me . . ., it nevertheless does not seem to me greater if I consider it formally and precisely in itself.[30]

Descartes also articulated a process—albeit an erroneous one—by which the mind exercises its will by causing changes in the brain, which then influence behavior. As I stated earlier, he proposed that the pineal gland serves as the intermediary between the mind and the brain. His own description of the process is contained in *The Passions of the Soul,* where he says, "And the whole action of the soul consists in this, that solely because it desires something, it causes the little gland to which it is closely united to move in the way requisite to produce the effect which relates to this desire."[31] Descartes' philosophy put human freedom on a par with God's, while it put the human mind in charge of human actions.

Philosophers still struggle with the concept of free will.[32] How can there be true freedom when, from physics, we could predict everything that happens if only we had enough data about the relevant molecules and atoms, including their exact locations, movements, and energy states. A modern authority on the subject of free will, Thomas Pink, refers it as "one of the very oldest and hardest problems in philosophy."[33] After reviewing various theories and arguments, Pink sides with the medieval philosopher, Thomas Aquinas, who said that above all else one must understand that the whole system of human morality depends on us believing in freedom of the will. Hence, freedom of the will is something that we *must* believe in whether true or not. Pink further endorses Aquinas's view that with freedom comes responsibility. In the following passage, Pink addresses what he sees as the difference between causation and freedom of the will.

> By contrast to causation, freedom seems limited to humans, or to at most humans and the higher animals. Freedom is unlike anything outside the mind in wider nature. But then the same is also true of many other features of the mind, such as our consciousness, our rationality, and our very capacity to understand. Yet all these, having control of what we do, being conscious, understanding things, are aspects of ourselves of which we are directly aware—as aware as we ever are of anything. Human freedom is certainly as puzzling and distinctive a phenomenon as any other of these features of our mentality. But it seems no less worthy of our belief than any of these others—a belief that we in any case seem perfectly incapable of abandoning.[34]

In the contorted passage quoted above, Pink seems to be saying that the will controls what we do, not by the usual means of causation but rather by virtue of its "puzzling and distinctive" features. He links human will with the human mind, and he invokes Cartesian dualism, even though the name Réne Descartes does not appear anywhere in the book. It is pertinent to note that Pink intended his book as a short introduction for the general reader, and the author repeatedly asserts that he is merely providing a sophisticated account of what most people already believe.

I think that Descartes, Aquinas, and Pink all speak for the population at large when they assert that personal freedom is an aspect of mind. Obviously, if only we humans are capable of exercising free will, by virtue of our unique minds, then we are indeed privileged. The downside, however, is that we become responsible for our actions. When we are held responsible for unconventional and bizarre behaviors, moral therapies of the type practiced by William Tuke and Philippe Pinel may be deemed appropriate. Even when such behaviors are seen as the result of a mental illness, the victim may still be held responsible and stigmatization can follow.

The close association of mental illness with moral responsibility has been noted by contemporary philosophers. For example, Christopher Boorse writes, "The puzzle about mental illness is that it seems to be an activity of the very seat of responsibility—the mind and character— and therefore to be beyond all hope of excuse."[35]

When bad things happen, the natural response is to look for *some one* to blame; less often do we blame *some thing*. This is one conclusion expressed by the American social psychologist, Bernard Weiner, in his influential book, *Judgments of Responsibility*.[36] Weiner emphasizes the natural tendency to attribute bad events to the willful actions of *people*, not to the actions of animals, the weather, or chance. This bias, he says, is related to the tendency to see *intentionality* in activity, even when that activity involves only inanimate objects.[37] Illnesses *per se* are not events, but the occasion when someone acquires an illness can be construed as an event. This possibility led Weiner to express another important conclusion, namely, that when a particular illness is consistently seen to result from personal failings, that illness becomes associated with stigma. Most moral judgments, according to Bernard Weiner, are based on assumptions of personal responsibility. When individuals are held responsible for their illnesses, they are judged poorly, and such moral judgments contribute to stigmas. "In sum," he says, "reactions to the stigmatized [individuals] are, in part, based on moral evaluations. Stigmatized persons considered responsible for their marks [stigmas] are construed as moral failures, which generates morality-related negative effects and, in turn, uncooperative behaviors."[38]

Weiner developed a framework to describe the process of assigning responsibility, whether for illness or for any other misfortune. He proposed that it begins with someone confirming that a particular event is caused by a particular person. Next, the individual who is assigning responsibility establishes that the cause in question was of such a nature that it was *internal to the actor* and *controllable*; in other words, it was a *willful* act. The final issue to be resolved is whether there are mitigating circumstances, such as moral justification, that could lessen or eliminate responsibility; if not, the person under scrutiny is said to be responsible for the event.

Weiner reminds us that, in the past, illnesses were often regarded as punishments for wrongdoings. To find out whether individuals today are still held responsible for their suffering, Weiner searched the scholarly literature. He found six studies that investigated how people distinguish different types of physical diseases.[39] Collectively, these studies identified two key properties that, in the minds of the public, distinguish various diseases. The first property is the severity of the symptoms. The second property, surprisingly, is the extent to which individuals are seen to be personally responsible for either getting the illness or controlling its outcome.

To further back up his hypothesis that assignments of personal responsibility generate stigma, Weiner cites a study that examined the characteristics of illnesses that cause people to shy away from, or reject, the victims. Crandall and Moriarty[40] asked subjects to rate sixty-six physical illnesses, ranging alphabetically from acne to whooping cough, on thirteen-scaled dimensions such as acute/chronic, severe/mild, hereditary/not hereditary, highly contagious/not at all contagious, etc. Each dimension was rated on a seven-point scale. The subjects were also asked to what extent they would reject individuals with each of the illnesses. The results showed that the attributes most highly correlated with social rejection were "caught by behavior" (meaning that the disease is caught by the person's behavior) and "avoidable" (meaning that the person could have avoided becoming ill). These data appear to support the idea that the perception of responsibility is a major determinant of social rejection. In the words of the authors, "The more a disease is perceived to be under volitional control, the more it is stigmatizing."[41] Significantly, as noted earlier, there is a tradition in psychiatry and within the greater society to view mental illnesses as "voluntary."

In another study, Weiner and colleagues asked people to rate ten stigmatized disorders according to how much responsibility should be assigned to those affected by the stigma.[42] The investigators characterized some of the disorders as "physical," for example, blindness, cancer, heart disease, and paraplegia, and others as "behavioral/mental," for example, child abuse, drug abuse, and obesity. Unfortunately, no unambiguous psychiatric illnesses were rated. Nevertheless, the investigators found that persons with the so-called behavioral/mental disorders were typically seen as responsible and blameworthy, whereas persons with physical disorders were seldom seen as responsible or blameworthy.

One final study sheds light on how mental health professionals render judgments of responsibility. Drs. Miresco and Kirmayer asked a group of psychiatrists and psychologists at the Department of Psychiatry of McGill University to read short vignettes.[43] The investigators told the participants that each vignette represented one of three different clinical conditions: (1) a manic episode induced by drug treatment, (2) a narcissistic personality disorder, or (3) a heroin dependency. As part of the experimental design, these three conditions were crossed with three descriptions of troubling behaviors, yielding a total of nine vignettes. After a participant had read a vignette, he or she was interrogated to probe his or her assignments of responsibility, along with related issues. The interesting result is that the more a fictional behavior was judged to have a *psychological* cause, the greater was the attribution of patient responsibility; conversely, the more a behavior was seen as having a *biological* cause, the less was the attribution of responsibility. The authors interpreted the results to imply that "mental health professionals employ a mind–brain dichotomy when reasoning about clinical cases." They urged their psychiatric colleagues "to consider carefully the potential implications of this kind of reasoning."[44]

Some Consequences of Attributed Responsibility

I have described how dualism fuels attributions of responsibility, which then contribute to the creation of mental illness stigma. While the harmful consequences of stigma are well known and have been reviewed above (loss of jobs, loss of friends, reluctance to seek professional help), other consequences of attributed responsibility are less obvious. Consider, for example, the doctor–patient relationship. Bernard Weiner thinks that "the quality of medical care may in part depend on the moral evaluation of the patient."[45] He cites a study in which medical students were asked whether they would prescribe tranquilizing drugs to fictional patients who were described as experiencing psychological stress.[46] The stress was the same in every case, but the cause of the stress varied, for example, divorce, loss of job, death in the family, etc. In addition to saying whether they would prescribe drugs, the students were required to rate each cause according to how likely it was that the patient could control it.

The results show that the students were more willing to prescribe drugs for conditions that they felt were *un*controllable than for conditions that they felt were controllable. The student doctors evidently assumed that the patients who were capable of resolving their own problems did not need drugs. Extrapolating from this study to real life, one might infer that when doctors think of mental illnesses as "controllable" or "voluntary," they will not be inclined to administer medications or other biological therapies.

Another result of attributed responsibility is the idea that mental patients can resolve their own problems and should be held responsible for doing so. This notion was a foundational belief of the moral therapists, but even today some patients and some family members welcome the suggestion that individuals cause their own illnesses; it gives them reason to believe that the process can be reversed. If the illness is caused in the first place by acts (or omissions) of the free will, then perhaps other willful acts (or omissions) can overcome or undo the illness. Ten percent of the respondents in a recent poll felt that persons with mental disorders can simply "snap out of it if they really wanted to."[47] Unfortunately, this is not true. While dualistic thinking fosters optimistic ideas by promoting the notion of "mind over matter," the reality is that to encourage self-healing is to raise false hopes and invite disappointments.

Up until the reforms of the late nineteenth century, the mentally ill were commonly mistreated. An assortment of brutalizing physical interventions sometimes masqueraded as therapies, whereas at other times they were simply recognized as moral necessities.[48] In light of the preceding discussion, it would be fair to assume that many, if not most, of these dehumanizing practices were the products of assigned responsibility. If the madman is morally responsible for his bizarre and unsociable behavior, should he not be punished? Even today, it is doubtless true that some mental patients in some institutions are cared for in a manner that lacks respect, to say the least. These practices, too, might derive from a punitive motive. Other treatments are *seen* as punishments when, in fact, they are not. A fascinating example is electroconvulsive treatment (ECT). After Ken Kesey vilified it in his 1962 novel, *One Flew Over the Cuckoo's Nest*, ECT became emblematic of the inhumane treatment of mental patients. The negative perception of ECT was further enhanced by its vivid portrayal in the 1975 film based on the book. Contrary to public opinion, however, ECT is actually a safe, painless, and effective treatment for major depression.[49]

Misinformation accounts for a large part of the discrepancy between popular understanding and medical reality, but two additional factors can be noted. First, the name *electroconvulsion* is already unfortunate because it connotes an uncontrolled, violent procedure, whereas the actual procedure is measured, closely monitored, and carried out under effective anesthesia. Second, and more interesting, it is likely that a poorly informed public is prepared to believe that mental patients are mistreated because—to put it bluntly—they deserve it. The reaction to ECT reflects, I think, the unspoken expectation that mental patients will be punished.

Finally, judgments of responsibility and judgments of mental competence are intertwined processes in the criminal law with important consequences for the accused individual. Although the law ordinarily holds people responsible for the acts that they commit, it makes an exception for persons who are severely mentally ill or, in legal terminology, insane. In most countries, the perpetrator of a crime is excused from punishment if he or she is found insane, following the precedent of the M'Naghten rule from Britain. The rule was introduced after a Scotsman, Daniel M'Naghten, had killed the secretary to the British Prime Minister. In responding to this case, the House of Lords established a new rule of law in 1844. Its purpose was to instruct courts in handling similar cases that might arise in the future. The M'Naghten rule states,

> Every man is to be presumed to be sane, and . . . that to establish a defense on the ground of insanity, it must be clearly proved that, at the time of the committing of the act, the party accused was laboring under such a defect of reason, from disease of mind, as not to know the nature and quality of the act he was doing; or if he did know it, that he did not know he was doing what was wrong.

The M'Naghten rule (with modernizations) is still the most common basis for acquittal by reason of mental illness. Nevertheless, a sizeable proportion of public opinion is firmly opposed to it. The case of John Hinkley in the United States is instructive. Hinkley successfully pleaded the insanity defense in his trial for the attempted murder of President Ronald Reagan, but one day after his acquittal, a nationwide poll found that 83 percent of Americans thought that "justice had not been done."[50]

More recently, in Canada, Vincent Li was traveling on a Greyhound bus in Manitoba when he moved to the back of the bus and sat down next to a stranger. He mumbled incoherently to himself for a few minutes, then pulled out a large knife and killed the young man. After stabbing him repeatedly, Mr. Li beheaded his victim and desecrated the body. At the trial, psychiatrists testifying for both the defense *and* the prosecution stated that Mr. Li had acted while under the influence of a major psychotic episode. Both sides asked the judge to declare Mr. Li not criminally responsible, and they recommended that he be sent to a psychiatric institution for treatment rather than to a prison for punishment (there is no death penalty in Canada). The judge followed their recommendation. As soon as news of the verdict was announced, however, radio talk shows were flooded with irate citizens demanding that, *regardless* of Mr. Li's mental condition, he should be incarcerated. The victim's mother, Carol de Delley, pleaded that it was "not acceptable" for Mr. Li to escape punishment. "The question," she said, "has become: treatment or punishment? I think it needs to be both." She also said, "So, he's not criminally responsible. Is he morally responsible then? He did kill an innocent man regardless of what drove him to it. If he walks the streets again, justice will not have been served."[51]

The cases of John Hickley and Vincent Li highlight the difference between the legal concept of responsibility and the commonplace, folk concept of responsibility. Legal opinion recognizes the power of delusions and hallucinations to cause acts of violence and, when the facts of a case warrant it, courts will absolve the accused of responsibility. Meanwhile, the public generally refuses to accept mental illness as an excuse. In their eyes, even an individual with a severe psychosis remains morally responsible and hence, punishable.

Can Stigma Be Eliminated?

Given that mental illness stigma is harmful, can anything be done about it? Some commentators believe that stigma will only disappear once the illnesses themselves disappear. These people push for programs of prevention and programs to "treat the stigma away." Others say that since nothing much can be done about it, we should focus instead on securing social justice for those affected by mental illness.[52] However, the most widely endorsed strategy is public education.

Current educational campaigns address the problem of stigma by emphasizing the biological basis of mental illness. The rationale for this approach is that by establishing a biological cause (genes, chemicals, brain alterations), people will be less inclined to consider the disorders voluntary. The approach makes sense if one believes, as I do, that one cause of stigma is the attribution of responsibility. Thus, the National Alliance on Mental Illness,[53] a large grassroots organization in the United States, says, "Just as diabetes is a disorder of the pancreas, mental illnesses are medical conditions." It further declares, "Schizophrenia is a disorder of the brain, caused by problems with brain chemistry and brain structure," and "Depression is not a flaw in character. It is a flaw in chemicals." Similarly, the World Psychiatric Association[54] runs an antistigma initiative under the banner "Open the Doors" that defines schizophrenia as "a brain disorder that affects the chemistry, structure, and function of the brain."

Although well intended, the educational campaigns have not been effective in lessening stigma. In fact, surveys in the United States, Germany, and elsewhere indicate that the desire to distance oneself from individuals with mental illness actually *increased* at the same time that knowledge of mental illnesses increased.[55] The American study compared data from two large-scale surveys conducted ten years apart. The surprising results led the authors to conclude,

> in surveys from both 1996 and 2006 . . . holding a neurobiological conception of mental illness either was unrelated to stigma or tended to increase the odds of a stigmatizing reaction. Our most striking finding is that stigma among the American public appears to be surprisingly fixed, even in the face of anticipated advances in public knowledge.[56]
>
> The "disease like any other" tagline has taken clinical and policy efforts far but is not without problems. It is our contention that future stigma reduction efforts need to be reconfigured or at least supplemented. An overreliance on the neurobiological causes of mental illness and substance use disorders is at best ineffective and at worst potentially stigmatizing.[57]

Some investigators surmise that the persistence of stigma is due to the persisting fear of violence. This may be true, but one needs to consider the role of the media. While mental health advocates campaign to educate the public about mental illness, the commercial media engage in parallel efforts to sell their products based on lurid stories of violence, some of which are associated with mental illness. Since no one has measured or disentangled the opposing effects of these two promotions, it is entirely possible that the educational campaign *would be* winning the battle against stigma if it were not for the increased awareness of violence brought about by media attention.

I favor a more ambitious educational campaign, one designed to combat stigma by reducing attributions of responsibility. First, the issue of violence needs to be confronted directly and with due attention to the facts. In particular, it must be emphasized that mental illness alone—even in cases of major psychosis—rarely causes violence. Second, and crucially, the educational message should aim to modernize concepts of mind and body. It is not enough to simply repeat the line that mental illness is "a disease like any other." I propose an educational program that addresses the intellectual shortcomings of dualism while suggesting instead an alternative philosophy grounded in modern science. An essential component of this campaign should be improved education about science. In particular, neuroscience has to be taught at a level of sophistication not yet attempted on a broad scale. Only when people fully grasp that nervous activity generates *all* of our mental life, including consciousness and other common subjective experiences, can we expect relief from the idea that the mind, as a substance distinct from the brain, is responsible for mental illness. I hasten to acknowledge that my plan to conquer the stigma of mental illness is anything but trivial. It may even be entirely unrealistic. Nevertheless, since there is no harm in trying, I will devote the remainder of this book to the effort.

Summary and Forward Glance

The stigma of mental illness is a complex phenomenon, which I have discussed only to highlight the role played by Cartesian dualism.[58] Dualistic assumptions work unconsciously to influence how we see things and how we respond to situations. In respect to mental illness, dualism promotes an exaggerated sense of free will which encourages attributions of personal responsibility. The attributions of personal responsibility lead to the moral judgments that cause stigmatization.

The shortcomings of the educational campaigns intended to combat stigma give pause for considering what, exactly, people understand when they are told that a mental illness is a disease of the brain. How do they reconcile this information with their tacit dualism? Earlier, I noted that it is possible to hold seemingly inconsistent views when factual knowledge is at odds with tacit assumptions. In the present case, I believe that people will accept, as intellectual fact, that mental illness has biological causes while continuing to believe, from intuition, that mental illness is voluntary. Cartesian dualism provides the context for maintaining both ideas because it posits two levels of control over behavior: first, the mind controls the brain, and second, the brain controls behavior. Thus, while problems in the brain may be responsible for mental illness, in the proximal sense, problems in the mind remain the ultimate cause. Seen from this perspective, a dualist might interpret information about the biology of mental illness as nothing other than evidence that mental illness is *real*; in other words, that it is something that is subject to scientific scrutiny. This same dualist will continue to believe that it is mental actions which cause the brain to become mis-wired or deficient in certain molecules. The cross-cultural work of Shweder *et al.* lends support to the idea that people are not entirely consistent in their thinking about illnesses because they found that people who attributed their illnesses to an interpersonal or moral cause were very often the same people who sought biomedical remedies.[59]

So far, while I have criticized Cartesian dualism, I have had little to say about alternative philosophies of mind. Is there a better philosophy, one that is logically consistent, compatible with modern science, and yet true to our intuitions? We will look at some options in the next chapter.

Notes

1. Pinel used the phrase "le traitement moral." According to the historian Edward Shorter, English speakers of the time translated the phrase as "moral therapy." See Shorter, 1997, pp. 19–20.
2. Ibid., p. 21.
3. See chapter 6.
4. Harris/NAMI survey, http://www.nami.org/sstemplate.cfm?section=Sch izophreniaSurvey.
5. National Report Card on Health Care, http://www.cma.ca/multimedia/ CMA/Content_Images/Inside_cma/Annual_Meeting/2008/GC_Bulletin/ National_Report_Card_EN.pdf.
6. Nordt et al., 2006.
7. Littlewood, 1998.
8. Surgeon General's Report on Mental Health, chapter 1. http://www. surgeongeneral.gov/library/mentalhealth/chapter1/sec1.html#roots_ stigma.
9. Montreal Gazette, http://www.montrealgazette.com/Health/Employers+ could+save+billions+reducing+stigma+mental+illness/1149411/story. html.
10. Gallo, 1994, p. 407.
11. Broucek, 1991, chapter 10.
12. For a comprehensive treatment of the stigma associated with mental illness, see Hinshaw, 2007.
13. Pescosolido et al., 2010.

14. Link et al., 1999; Angermeyer and Matschinger, 2005.
15. Surgeon General's Report on Mental Health, chapter 1. http://www.surgeongeneral.gov/library/mentalhealth/chapter1/sec1.html#roots_stigma.
16. Elbogen and Johnson, 2009.
17. Link et al., 1999.
18. Foucault, 1965.
19. Porter, 1987, p. 279.
20. Kim and Berrios, 2001.
21. Kim and Berrios, 2001; Takahashi et al., 2009.
22. Takahashi et al., 2009.
23. Quoted in Link et al., 1999, p. 1331.
24. Surgeon General's Report on Mental Health, chapter 1. http://www.surgeongeneral.gov/library/mentalhealth/chapter1/sec1.html#roots_stigma.
25. Shweder et al., 1997.
26. Ibid., p. 125.
27. Ibid., p. 130.
28. Ibid., p. 122–23.
29. Ibid., p. 120.
30. Descartes, 1641, Meditation IV. See Descartes, 1965.
31. Descartes, 1650, Part one, article XLI. See Descartes, 1965.
32. For a critical discussion of free will, see Dennett, 1984.
33. Pink, 2004, p. 2.
34. Ibid., p. 123.
35. Boorse, 1975, p. 66.
36. Weiner, 1995.
37. In chapter 3, p. 36, I described movies in which squares appeared to bully circles.
38. Weiner, 1995, p. 65.
39. Ibid., pp. 58–61.
40. Crandall and Moriarty, 1995.
41. Ibid., p. 72.
42. Weiner et al., 1988.
43. Miresco and Kirmayer, 2006.
44. Ibid., pp. 917–18.
45. Weiner, 1995, p. 61.
46. Brewin, 1984.
47. Survey by the Canadian Medical Association, 2008; see chapter 2, p. 18.
48. For details, see Shorter, 1997.
49. Shorter and Healy, 2007.
50. http://www.law.umkc.edu/faculty/projects/ftrials/hinckley/hinckleytrial.html.
51. http://www.cbc.ca/canada/manitoba/story/2008/10/09/de-delley.html.
52. Corrigan et al., 2005.
53. http://www.nami.org/.
54. http://www.wpanet.org/.
55. Angermeyer and Matschinger, 2005; Pescosolido et al., 2010.

56.   Pescosolido et al., 2010, p. 1325.
57.   Ibid., p. 1327.
58.   For a complete account of stigma, see Hinshaw, 2007.
59.   Shweder et al., 1997, p. 128. See my discussion of their study on p. 59.

5

Philosophical Alternatives to Cartesian Dualism

Up until now, I have presented only a single view of the mind in much detail, namely Cartesian dualism. As we have seen, the main elements of this philosophy are, first, that mind and body are two distinct "substances," and second, that interactions occur between mind and body such that the mind can influence the body. People who adopt this philosophy of mind will tend to believe that mental illnesses are, literally, illness of the mind. We know, however, that philosophers and neuroscientists have serious doubts about the validity of Cartesian dualism. If these criticisms are accepted, we need another philosophy to answer the persistent question, what is mind? Most of us imagine that it is *something* because we speak of it a lot and it enters into our folk psychology, but how does one think sensibly about it?

If there were an easy answer to what mind is, there would be far fewer professors of philosophy, nothing like the 500 scholarly articles published on the topic since 1993,[1] and certainly not the 40,000 books that outrageously appear when Amazon.com is searched for "philosophy of mind." Searched with the same key words, the library catalogue at my university coughs up 459 titles. The problems under scrutiny are extremely challenging, and there are no experiments that can *prove* the truth or falsity of any metaphysical proposition. So, the arguments tend to go on and on, with only cold logic available to freeze out nonsense and speculation. In reflecting on the current status of academic philosophy of mind, the editors of *The Oxford Handbook of Philosophy of Mind* wrote this in the introduction to their 800 page book:

> Virtually all of the essays [in this book] note that one or another issue in the philosophy of mind remains unresolved. Indeed, fundamental issues in the philosophy of mind remain unresolved . . . . Positions defended in one essay are sometimes attacked in another;

a presupposition of one essay is sometimes challenged in another; a problem presented as insuperable in one essay is sometimes claimed in another to be resolvable; in some cases there is an important question whether a position taken in one essay is in conflict with a position taken in another.[2]

The above confession of professional inadequacy is refreshing, and it sounds a cautionary note. The ideas debated in the philosophy of mind are sometimes subtle, sometimes complex, and often both subtle *and* complex. If we should become frustrated in our efforts to understand, we can take solace in the perspective of Jaegwon Kim, one of the leading philosophers of mind:

> Why should we suppose that all problems are solvable—and solvable by us? (Just because we find difficult, perhaps insoluble, moral problems and puzzles, should we cast aside moral concepts and moral discourse?) It may well be that our mind–body problem, or something close to it, arises within any scheme that is rich enough to do justice to the world as we experience it. It may well be that the problem is an inexorable consequence of the tension between the objective world of physical existence and the subjective world of experience, and that the distinction between the objective and the subjective is unavoidable for reflective cognizers and agents of the kind that we are.[3]

In the first part of this chapter, I will provide a survey of theories to illustrate the clever ways in which philosophers have approached the mind–body problem since the time of Descartes. Then I will focus on two key issues that especially relate to mental illness: whether mind is anything more than brain, and whether mind can cause things to happen. Although I would not be so foolish as to declare any theory "true" or any proposed resolution of an issue "correct," I will venture my evaluations at the end of each section.

Inspired By Descartes

Descartes deserves the credit, or blame, for igniting the flames of metaphysical argument that still burn today. The heat began even before he died. Shortly after he published his most influential works, other authors announced their own philosophies of mind. Some authors accepted Cartesian dualism, others tinkered with it, and still others abandoned dualism altogether for monism. George Berkeley's (1685–1753) response was especially radical. His position, known as *idealism*, was an updated version of Plato's metaphysics. Neither he nor Plato believed that the physical world exists. The world that appears physical is nothing but a construction of our senses and our thoughts. Hence, idealism is a type of monism in which only mind exists. Berkeley never actually posed the question whether a tree falling in an uninhabited forest makes a sound, but this famous conundrum does capture the essence of his ideas because, according to him, if one neither *hears* the sound *nor thinks* about the sound, it does not exist. Like the other theories of mind to be discussed here, idealism has had its proponents as well as its critics. Immanuel Kant (1724–1804) and Georg Wilhelm Friedrich Hegel (1770–1831) were idealists, and so too is the contemporary philosopher, Howard Robinson. An especially original version of idealism was proposed by Gottfried Wilhelm Leibniz (1646–1716). He believed that the natural world is constituted of very many units of being, which he called *monads*. Since Leibniz assumed that each monad has properties similar to those that we attribute to mind, his metaphysical philosophy is a type of idealism in which mind is everywhere and there is nothing but mind.

Other interesting theories grew out of the attempts to rescue Cartesian dualism from its main defect, the implausibility of the mind influencing the brain. Nicolas de Malebranche (1638–1715), for example, was motivated to propose the curious theory of *occasionalism*. Because God is the source of all causes, Malebranche wrote, he must be involved every time something happens. Therefore, it is neither necessary nor true that the mind causes changes in the brain. Rather, on every occasion when this *seems* to be the case, what is really happening is that God is intervening to cause appropriate and simultaneous changes in both mind and brain. A related idea, *parallelism*, was put forward by two other contemporaries of Descartes, Leibniz and Arnold Geulincx (1625–99). As mentioned above, Leibniz was an idealist who believed that mind-like monads are the fundamental elements of reality. He imagined that each monad operates independently of all other monads. Therefore, no (ordinary) causation occurs anywhere in the universe because there are no interactions among the monads; likewise, the mind and the brain do not interact. Geulincx framed his notion of parallelism somewhat differently from Leibniz because he thought, like Descartes, that the mind and the brain are both substances. His idea was that the mind and the brain invariably act together (in parallel) because God had set up a pre-established harmony among all things when he created the world.

Two centuries later, Thomas Huxley (1825–95), a friend and supporter of Charles Darwin, came up with his own version of dualism. He accepted that physical events cause mental events, but he denied the opposite; mental events, he said, do not cause physical events. Rather, Huxley felt that the mind is an inconsequential by-product of the brain's activity, something totally incapable of influencing either the brain or behavior. Huxley said that the mind is like the steam that emerges from the chimney on a locomotive train: it contributes nothing to moving the vehicle. Today, we use the term *epiphenomenon* to describe the steam on the train, and Huxley's view of the mind is known as epiphenomenalism; the prefix *epi* means *beside*.

Evaluation. Because all the theories summarized above—occasionalism, parallelism, and epiphenomenalism—reject Descartes' assertions of mental causation, no follower of these theories would entertain the idea that psychiatric illnesses are caused by problems in the mind. The occasionalist and the parallelist would say that brain aberrations and mental aberrations occur together, but neither is caused by the other. The epiphenomenalist, alone, would be comfortable with the idea that brain abnormalities cause psychiatric illnesses. Thus, only epiphenomenalism fits well with modern scientific views on the nature and causes of mental illness. For my money, occasionalism and parallelism get marks for cleverness, but neither approaches credibility. Epiphenomenalism, on the other hand, has the ring of truth. Indeed, several contemporary philosophers have adopted epiphenomenalism as a general theory of mind, while others think that at least certain aspects of mind are epiphenomenal; I will have more to say about this later in the chapter.

Behaviorism: Making Do Without Mind

Some people find it convenient to discard the entire idea of the mind rather than try to incorporate it into a plausible description of the natural world. For them, the philosophy of *behaviorism* was an attractive choice until it fell out of favor towards the end of the twentieth century. Behaviorism is the complete opposite of idealism. Whereas idealism claims that *everything* is mind, behaviorism asserts that *nothing* is mind. The American psychologist, J.B. Watson, first argued this position in 1913. Watson was an experimental scientist who observed and measured the behaviors of rodents. He had no use for invisible phenomena like intentions, beliefs, feelings, or any of the stuff that constitutes human consciousness. Nor did Watson spend a lot of time thinking deeply about philosophical problems. Rather, he was interested in understanding and manipulating animal behavior, and for this purpose he preferred to think of behaviors as nothing other than responses to stimuli (stimulus–response psychology). Even the so-called "complex" behaviors, Watson wrote, are only long sequences of stimuli and responses to stimuli. Watson's ideas remained obscure until he (inevitably?) extended them from rats to humans, at which point they became controversial. After Watson's death, the Harvard psychologist, B.F. Skinner, took up the behaviorist program; his experimental subjects included not only rats, but also pigeons and humans. Skinner published a book called *Beyond Freedom and Dignity*, intended for public reading.[4] The title alone was enough to cause widespread outrage, for obvious reasons.

A different version of behaviorism, known as *logical behaviorism*, was adopted by Gilbert Ryle, whose dismissal of Cartesian dualism was briefly discussed in chapter 3. Ryle was a professor at Oxford University during the period when academic philosophers were busy analyzing the logical meanings of words and sentences (roughly from 1930 to 1950). In his famous book, *The Concept of Mind*,[5] Ryle focused on linguistic references to mind and behavior. He accepted the usefulness of mental terms for explaining behavior, but he insisted that talking (or writing) about mental actions is just another way of talking about bodily actions. He emphasized the equivalence of mental actions and bodily actions by pointing out that it is always possible to reformulate statements about mental events into "if . . . then" statements. For example, one can replace "Tom is thirsty" with "*If* Tom has had nothing to drink for the past two days, *then* he will accept my offer of water." In this example, and many others like it, Ryle explained that the language of observable behaviors (no drink for two days, accepts my offer) can easily replace the language of mental states (he is thirsty). Thus, from a strictly logical point of view, there is no need for mental terms. With all of his arguments, Ryle called attention to the logical implications of our everyday references to mental states and mental events. He concluded that we can manage quite well without using any concept of mind.

The philosophy of *eliminative materialism* cuts even more deeply into mental language and folk psychology. According to this philosophy, everything unrelated to material things should simply be eliminated from our speech and our thoughts. Clearly, there is no place for mind in this philosophy. Other versions of materialism allow that certain types of brain activity have mental properties as well as physical properties, as I will discuss below, but the eliminative materialists refuse to accept the existence of even mental properties. They maintain that all the common sense talk of ideas, beliefs, desires, feelings, etc. is nothing but conceptual rubbish. The husband-and-wife team of Paul and Patricia Churchland are prominent advocates of eliminative materialism.[6] Their knowledge of neuroscience and computer science leads them to say that folk psychology has completely failed to explain such phenomena as consciousness, memory, and mental illness, whereas science is beginning to make progress in these areas. Looking into the future, they envisage the day when serious investigators will no longer speak of human behaviors driven by love, revenge, ambition, or the like, but instead use a completely new manner of explanation. The Churchlands have not spelled out the exact nature of this new type of explanation, but they are confident that it will not involve any of the sentence-like explanations that are currently commonplace. It may include, they say, a "non-linguistic vector/matrix model of neural networks."

Evaluation. The eliminative materialists, the behaviorists, and the idealists, all take a radical position with respect to mind and body. Some people find these ideas appealing because they sweep away the metaphysical tension that Jaegwon Kim referred to in the passage quoted at the beginning of this chapter, leaving only mind or only matter. Recall, however, that Kim also said that "the distinction between the objective and the subjective is unavoidable." Most people, myself included, are unwilling to give up either the objective world or the subjective world. We need a philosophy of mind that recognizes both worlds, without falling back on substance dualism.

Physicalism: A Popular Choice

Physicalism, also known as *materialism,* is a theory of mind popular among both philosophers and ordinary folk. It was first introduced in 1933, not by a philosopher, but by a psychologist named Edwin Boring. Boring's textbook on the history of psychology was required reading when I was a graduate student; my fellow students joked that the subject had found its ideal author.

Physicalism is a monist philosophy because it says that everything in the world is a physical thing. Mental states and mental events are understood to be identical to brain states and brain events. However, physicalist philosophers disagree about exactly what *identical* means in this case. Those who adhere to the original version of the theory have a literal interpretation of identity, whereas those who accept a revised version have a somewhat looser interpretation, as I will explain. Regardless, physicalists are unanimous in saying that mental experience is totally dependent on brain activity. Most physicalists expect that neuroscientists will eventually be able to detail the physiological events that accompany episodes of consciousness, and solid progress has been made toward this objective.[7] However, even if scientists are successful in discovering the neuronal *correlates* of consciousness, that is, the specific brain events that are consistently associated with specific mental events, this will not be enough to explain *how* the physical brain generates subjective experiences. Many philosophers, including some physicalists, think that there is no solution to the latter mystery.

Rachel Cooper, the author of *Psychiatry and Philosophy of Science*, relates a chilling conversation to illustrate the meaning of physicalism.[8] The conversation was between a brain surgeon and his patient, and apparently it really happened. As is often the case in modern brain surgeries, the patient was conscious throughout the operation. At one point in the procedure, the surgeon asked the patient, "What's going through your mind?" After a long pause, the patient replied, "a knife," exactly as a physicalist should have replied.

The original version of physicalism (known as the identity theory) is illustrated by the nature of water. We know water by its many attributes, such as wetness, clarity, tastelessness, etc., but we also know it by its chemical formula, H2O. It is natural to think of the attributes as representing a *higher level* description and the chemical formula as representing a *lower level* description, but there is never an occasion when the word *water* cannot be replaced with *H2O*, and vice versa. Water and H2O have exactly the same meanings; they are identical. When philosophers speak of replacing a higher level description with a lower level description, they use the word *reduction.* By definition, reduction refers to the process of understanding complex things in terms of their simpler or more fundamental parts. Therefore, physicalism is fundamentally reductionist. Water is nothing but H2O, and *mind is nothing but matter.*

Physicalism initially faced a challenge from those who claimed to detect a logical fallacy. The standard illustration of the problem goes as follows. Many years ago, anatomists classified nerve fiber types according to their diameters. As it happens, the smallest diameter fibers, called C-fibers, are associated with pain. More precisely, whenever the C-fibers fire action potentials, a person feels pain, and whenever someone feels pain, the C-fibers are firing. The physicalists therefore proclaimed that pain and C-fiber firing are identical. The critics protested, however, saying that pain could not be identical to C-fiber firing because some animals feel pain yet have absolutely no C-fibers. Octopuses, for example, probably experience pain judging from their behaviors, but their nervous system is very different from our own, and they have no C-fibers. The critics say that the mental state (pain) is not equivalent to any single physical state (C-fiber firing), but to *different* physical states in *different* animals. More generally, they believe that no mental state is equivalent to any single physical state. Brain imaging studies in humans appear to confirm this by showing that certain mental states are correlated with different patterns of neural activity in different individuals.

In the jargon used by philosophers, pain is an example of *multiple realization*. The exact meaning of the term *realization* is elusive, but it refers to the supposed connection between higher level properties and lower level properties. Each higher level property is thought to be realized in a lower level property. Mental states, for example, are realized in various physical properties of the nervous system. The critics of physicalism assert that because pain is realized in many possible ways (multiply) within the nervous system, it cannot possibly be identical to any one physical state (in contrast to water and H2O). Therefore, in so far as the theory of physicalism relies on the identity of mind and brain, it must be wrong. Note also that the prospect of multiple realization poses a problem for physical (neurobiological) explanations of psychiatric conditions. Paranoia in one individual could be due to certain physiological changes in certain neurons, whereas paranoia in another individual might be caused by *other* physiological changes in *other* neurons.

Physicalists responded to the challenge of multiple realization by proposing a revised theory.[9] To appreciate the distinction between the original theory and the revised theory, think about *hurricanes*. Hurricanes are violent storms caused by large low-pressure systems and characterized by strong winds and heavy rainfalls. Each hurricane, however, is different in its particulars from every other one. Even if it were possible to measure precisely the size and distribution of air pressures, water droplets, and winds, one would never find any two hurricanes that fit exactly the same physical description. The identity of hurricanes with physical states, therefore, is unlike the identity of water with H2O. Nonetheless, say the physicalists, a hurricane is nothing but a physical state; given enough data, any particular hurricane can be completely described by its physics. Similarly, for any particular person with a particular paranoiac condition, there will be a unique physical realization. In other words, the condition can always be reduced to one specific alteration in brain circuitry and/ or brain physiology. Moreover, since most of the psychological and neurological features of paranoia are at least similar in all cases, it is possible to make some generalizations. For example, we can say that paranoia always involves the amygdala. If schizophrenia, depression, anxiety, etc. are likewise terms that describe particular types of mental states, each one will also be reducible, in most cases and at least partially, to a particular brain condition.

Evaluation. Physicalism draws strength from its roots in modern science, which is fundamentally materialistic and reductionistic. While it boldly squashes dualism by declaring that the mind is nothing over and above the brain, it is not a totally satisfying theory of mind. The revised version of physicalism meets the challenge of multiple realizability, but it leaves behind a more vigorous original version. Also, the revised version introduces the uncomfortable possibility that mental states such as pain might be realized in physical systems other than brains, even in computers, provided that they are made of the right stuff or constructed in the right way. Finally, physicalism does not adequately account for subjective experiences.

Functionalism: Clever but Fuzzy

Shortly after computing machines first appeared, Hilary Putnam, a philosopher at Harvard University, found himself spending a lot of time thinking about how they work. He realized that while different machines have different designs and different hardware, they all share the capacity to process information. Putnam began thinking of the computer's information processing tasks as *functions*, where each function involves the transformation of pieces of information. He paid attention to what information goes into a machine and what information comes out; from this, he constructed input-output functions. To take a very simple example, he would define multiplication as the relationship between an input (the numbers 4 and 5) and an output (20). To know what multiplication is, said Putnam, you do not have to know *how* the computer does it or *why* it does it. All you need to know is *what* the computer does: it transforms the numbers 4 and 5 to yield 20. Students of Putnam took this insight and applied it to mental phenomena such as pain. Pain, for philosophers such as Jerry Fodor, is simply a function that minimizes tissue damage.[10] Pain is completely described by its inputs, for example a bee sting, and by its outputs, for example moaning and running away. It is enough to know that pain has the same function in all humans and all animals, so we need not bother about *how* pain is produced, and the physicalists' concern with multiple realizability is nullified. *Functionalism* says that mental states such as pain, thirst, love, etc. are best characterized as functions.

Functionalism is not so much an alternative to physicalism as a supplement, since most functionalists believe that everything is ultimately physical. However, while physicalism per se stresses the identity of mind and brain, functionalism stresses the causal relationships between mental states and behavioral outputs, and between one mental state and another mental state. According to one authority, functionalism is "the dominant view of mind among philosophers,"[11] this despite the fact that it has little to say about consciousness.

The shortcomings of functionalism with respect to consciousness are well illustrated by one of the leading arguments against the theory. The argument consists of a thought experiment that invokes the notion of *inverted qualia* or *inverted spectra*. Qualia, it will be recalled, are the subjective, "qualitative," experiences that we have when we sense physical stimuli, whether of internal or external origins. Examples include the quale of tasting strawberries and the quale of smelling rose blossoms but the thought experiment that we will consider involves the qualia associated with colors. Because qualia are (quintessentially) mental states, they are presumed to have functions. Robert Van Gulick sets up the experiment, and the philosophical argument, by asking us to imagine two friends, Norm and Flip,

> who are totally alike in their functional organization but experience different qualia when they perceive a given sort of object. When they look at a lime, they both call it "green," and the inner states produced play the same functional role in each of them, but the quale associated with that state in Flip is the one associated with the states produced in Norm by ripe tomatoes.[12]

Note that "the inner states produced play the same functional role" in both Norm and Flip. This means that the same defined stimulus elicits the same defined response in both individuals. Functionalist philosophy holds that mental states are defined by their functions. The problem posed by the thought experiment is that two different mental states, those associated with seeing red and seeing green, are both associated with the same function. Thus, the functional definition fails to capture the distinctive subjective qualities of seeing-red and seeing-green. Regardless of whether any two individuals actually have inverted spectra, even to conceive of the situation is enough, say the critics, to prove the nonfunctionality of qualia.

On the other side of the argument, Daniel Dennett is one of several well-known philosophers who dismiss the possibility of inverted qualia; he refers to the idea as "philosophical fantasy." In his book *Consciousness Explained*,[13] Dennett takes the position that, in fact, there are no qualia at all, only "dispositions to react." Qualia are simply illusions based on faulty intuitions, things that people talk about but which do not actually exist. He acknowledges, of course, that we respond differently to different colors, different odors, etc., but he concludes from this only that stimulus information is processed and behavioral reactions are subject to certain internal dispositions.

Like physicalism, functionalism also carries the bizarre implication that machines may have mental lives. Because it is possible to construct robots that can sense damage and take actions to avoid further damage, it is conceivable, say the functionalists, that robots have pains. Some functionalists even go so far as to say that any machine performing a function has intentions and experiences sensory stimulation (i.e., has qualia). Moreover, since a given function remains the same regardless of how it is realized in a living body or a machine, a machine need not be fancy in order to be conscious. One functionalist philosopher, David Chalmers, has famously proposed that even an ordinary home thermostat could be conscious because it exhibits the function of maintaining a constant temperature. In a section of his book titled "What is it like to be a thermostat?", Chalmers speculates on the conscious life of thermostats.

> Certainly it will not be very interesting to be a thermostat. The information processing is so simple that we should expect the corresponding phenomenal states to be equally simple .... Perhaps we can think of these states by analogy to our experiences of black, white, and gray: a thermostat can have an all-black phenomenal field, an all-white field, or an all-gray field. But even this is to impute far too much structure to the thermostat's experiences, by suggesting

the dimensionality of a visual field, and the relatively rich natures of black, white, and gray. We should really expect something much simpler, for which there is no analog in our experience. We will likely be unable to sympathetically imagine these experiences any better than a blind person can imagine sight, or than a human can imagine what it is like to be a bat; but we can at least intellectually know something about their basic structure.[14]

Chalmers's hypothesis about thermostats with "phenomenal states" and "experiences" suggests a form of *panpsychism* according to which all things that process information, and therefore have functions, have consciousness. Maybe he isn't entirely convinced of this, but he does write as though he takes the idea seriously.[15]

Evaluation. I begin with Chalmers's speculation about doorknobs. While drawing deserved attention to the clever ideas inherent in functional theory, the notion of conscious doorknobs has been the target of ridicule. As far as I am concerned, I care not whether the phenomenal states of the doorknob are simple or complex. My concern is whether the doorknob has any phenomenal states at all, and I do not believe that it does.

Functionalism also introduces a troubling implication for psychiatry. Functionalists invite us to think of the mind as the software that runs on the hardware of the brain.[16] This view has consequences for psychiatry because, as Rachel Cooper points out, "If functionalism is adopted as an account of mind, one implication is that we should expect human beings to be vulnerable to two types of mental disorder. Some would be caused by problems with the hardware of the brain. Others would be caused by problems in the 'software' of the mind."[17] Therefore, to adopt functionalism is to double the challenge of diagnosis and treatment.

Because functionalism does not attempt to reduce mental phenomena to physical phenomena, it gives us license to talk about thoughts and feelings as states of mind with causal powers. This is an improvement over physicalism. However, functionalism comes up short in offering any perspective on what mind actually *is*. Mind, for the functionalists, is simply a collection of functions. Physicalism, on the other hand, reduces the mental to the physical, so it too offers no satisfactory account of the mental life. In this circumstance, given the choice between the two pillars of modern philosophy of mind, physicalism and functionalism, many people look for a third way, a conceptualization that recognizes the primacy of the physical world while at the same time acknowledging the reality of our mental experiences. Some helpful ideas along these lines will be discussed in my closing chapter.

Are Mental States Reducible?

One of the overarching questions in the philosophy of mind is whether mental states can be reduced to brain states. Reduction, you will recall, involves thinking about complex things in terms of their simpler components. Some of the confusion about mental illness might disappear if we could relinquish the notion of a strange condition affecting a complex, unknowable mind, and accept that it is an abnormality affecting nerve cells and molecules. However, the concept of reduction is itself complex. Rachel Cooper identifies three different uses of the term reduction, depending on the purpose.[18] It will be useful to bear in mind the following definitions because they enter into subsequent discussions. *Metaphysical reduction* is about what exists in the world; when successful, it demonstrates that higher level phenomena (like the mind) are nothing over and above lower level phenomena (like the brain). *Explanatory reduction* (also called *epistemic reduction*) is concerned less about the nature of things than about what works as an explanation of psychological and mental phenomena; it seeks explanations in the neurobiological sciences. Finally, *methodological reduction* is a strategy that scientists employ when designing experiments; it results in scientists working with the smallest possible entities, for example, atoms rather than rocks, and cells rather than brains.

How do the different types of reduction relate to the mind–body problem in philosophy? Here are some examples. When someone says that mental illnesses are brain illnesses, he or she is certainly using explanatory reduction and may also be using metaphysical reduction. When a geneticist designs a study to look for genes associated with schizophrenia, she is using methodological reduction in order to obtain statistically significant results. Mind–body dualists obviously reject metaphysical reduction, and they generally reject explanatory reduction, but they often accept methodological reduction. Most physicalists accept all three types of reduction, but some are prepared to make exceptions for certain types of mental activities. Perhaps, they say, not *everything* can be reduced to physics. Prominent among this group of dissatisfied physicalists is Donald Davidson, whose important work warrants our attention.

Davidson was a professor of philosophy at Stanford University and the University of California until his death in 2003. Basically, he was a physicalist who believed that only matter exists. Nevertheless, he maintained that psychological explanations cannot be reduced to neurobiological explanations. Davidson, therefore, was a metaphysical reductionist but not an explanatory reductionist. His philosophy of mind is called *anomalous monism*,[19] a term whose meaning will become clear after I first consider some details of the theory.

Davidson built his philosophy on the concept of *mental properties*, which references things that cannot be described in purely physical language. Davidson maintained that mental properties grow out of, or emerge from, brain activities. To explain the nature of mental properties and their relationship to physical properties, Davidson borrowed from the philosophical principle of *supervenience*, which states that in some situations a set of properties (here, the mental) can be "higher" than another set (here, the physical), and crucially, properties in the higher set are completely dependent on properties in the lower set. Thus, if we understand the mind–brain relationship as one of supervenience, any change in the brain must result in a change in the mind. Also, if two mental states have different properties, the corresponding brain states must also differ. Neither of these constraints, however, disallows the possibility that the same mental state could be dependent on two different brain states. This last feature is important because, like multiple realizability, it thwarts efforts to identify mental states with brain states. However, supervenience alone is not enough to establish the irreducibility of mind.

Davidson introduced a totally new argument for the irreducibility of mental states to brain states. The crux of the argument is this: whereas reduction in the closed physical world involves the application of strict rules, there are no strict rules that can govern reductions from the mental world to the physical world; therefore, reductions from the mental to the physical are not possible. In her lucid explanation of Davidson's argument, Rachel Cooper uses examples to illustrate the impediments that prevent mental-to-physical reductions. She begins by inviting us to consider the difference between attributing mental states and attributing physical states.[20] As an example of physical attribution, consider how we determine someone's weight. Quite simply, we make a measurement. We put the person on a scale, the scale yields a number, and that number *is* the person's weight, period.

No other fact or measurement concerning that person can change this particular attribute unless, of course, it is a fact or measurement about the person's weight. One way to think of the relationship between the physical attribute (the person's weight) and the measured value (say, 150 pounds) is to call it *one-to-one*. Mental states, on the other hand, cannot be attributed on a one-to-one basis because they are open to revision. Rachel Cooper asks us to suppose that a woman turns on a water tap.

> What might we conclude from this? We probably conclude that she wants a drink of water and believes that water will come from the tap. But suppose we then hear her say "I'll need to take a sample of this." Then we might conclude that she believes the water has been contaminated and a sample needs to be taken. Can we stop here? No, because we might then learn that [she] believes herself to be in a play, then we would conclude that she is just pretending to take a sample. The point is that when we attribute beliefs and desires to [someone] we always have to be open to the possibility that we may have to revise them in the light of evidence concerning the [person's] other mental states.[21]

The need for revision "in the light of . . . other mental states" necessitates that mental states, in contrast to physical states, must be *attributed as sets*.

An additional feature of mental states that likewise requires their specification by sets is the requirement for every mental state to be consistent with every other mental state. For example, we might hear a woman say that she "loves cats," and later hear her say that she "hates cats." It would be wrong to assume that she both loves and hates cats because mental states are normally *rational*, and to both love and hate cats is clearly *irrational*. In this example, therefore, it might be that the woman's "love" comment was prompted by one particular cat, whereas the "hate" comment was prompted by a different cat. It would be quite rational to love some cats, but hate others. Physical states, by contrast, are not subject to the constraint of rationality.

According to Davidson, there can be no rules for reducing mental states to physical states because the two things (kinds of states) are fundamentally incompatible; one is attributed in sets, the other is attributed one-by-one. Thus, since there are no rules for reduction, at least some kinds of mental phenomena are irreducible. This is the essence of *anomalous monism*, where *monism* refers to physicalism and *anomalous* means without laws (Greek *nomo* = law). Therefore, anomalous monism translates as "physicalism with no laws for reduction."

David Chalmers, the Australian philosopher, rejects both the possibility of mental reduction and the broader idea of physicalism. I have already remarked on his contentious ideas about the conscious states of doorknobs. Equally outrageous, according to some commentators, is his zombie argument. Chalmers contends that human zombies might be possible. He speaks not of Hollywood's zombies but of those that would appear to be comfortable sitting in a philosopher's armchair—*except* that Chalmers's zombies are *never* comfortable, nor do they ever feel, believe, intend, or think anything. In Chalmers's book, *The Conscious Mind,* he asks us to imagine a twin who is identical to himself in every way except that he has no consciousness; in other words, the twin is a zombie.

> This creature is molecule for molecule identical to me, and identical in all the low-level properties postulated by a completed physics, but he lacks conscious experience entirely . . . . To fix ideas, we can imagine that right now I am gazing out the window, experiencing some nice green sensations from seeing the trees outside, having pleasant taste experiences through munching on a chocolate bar, and feeling a dull aching sensation in my right shoulder . . . . What is going on in my zombie twin? He is physically identical to me, and we may as well suppose that he is embedded in any identical environment. He will certainly be identical to me *functionally*: he will be processing the same sort of information, reacting in a similar way to inputs, with his internal configurations being modified appropriately and with indistinguishable behavior resulting . . . . He will be perceiving the trees outside, in the functional sense, and tasting the chocolate, in the psychological sense . . . . It is just that none of this functioning will be accompanied by any real conscious experience. There will be no phenomenal feel. There is nothing it is like to be a zombie.[22]

You will recall that, according to supervenience, any two brains that are physically identical must also be mentally identical. Chalmers is saying no, even if the brain of one twin (Chalmers's brain) produces consciousness, that says nothing about consciousness in the brain of the other twin (the zombie's brain). Therefore, says Chalmers, the supervenience principle does not apply to the mind–body issue. Contrary to supervenience, and physicalism generally, the mind is over and above the brain, and physical facts do not determine all facts. Moreover, he makes the stronger claim that it does not even matter whether zombies actually exist. Since he can "coherently conceive" of them, he says, they are logically possible, and if they are logically possible physicalism must be wrong. Chalmers does not treat consciousness as a substance, like Descartes did, but rather as the irreducible property of events or states that also have physical properties.

Chalmers's zombie argument is seductive, but it has met stiff opposition from critics who argue that even if *he* can conceive of a zombie twin, *they* cannot. His belief alone does not constitute a logical proof. The critics ask us to think about the nature of water. Just because a person who is ignorant of chemistry may conceive of water without H2O, that does not prove that water and H2O are different substances. In a review of Chalmers's book published in the *New York Review of Books*, the American philosopher John Searle wrote that while Chalmers could imagine zombies, he, Searle, could imagine "a world in which pigs can fly, and rocks are alive."[23] But, he adds, such a world would necessarily have different "laws of nature" than our familiar world. He insists that because our brains most certainly produce consciousness, zombies could exist only if they had brains different from ours. In short, most philosophers reject Chalmers's zombie argument.[24]

The status of qualia, discussed above in relation to functionalism, is central to the question of mind-to-brain reduction. One influential philosopher, Jaegwon Kim, believes that only functional mental events can be reduced to brain events, and since he accepts that qualia cannot be functional because of the inverted spectrum argument, he does not believe that qualia can be reduced to brain states.[25] Reflecting more generally on the reducibility of mind, Kim writes that

> we should not think that the mental as a totality is either reducible or irreducible; it may well be that part of the mental is reducible, though not all of it is. It may well be—I believe this to be the case – that intentional/cognitive states are physically reducible while phenomenal aspects of conscious experience, or "qualia," are not so reducible.[26]

A different opinion is offered by the neuroscientist, Christof Koch. He thinks that qualia are real, that they are "closely tied up with meaning," and that they are represented in the brain by a network of neurons. He comes to this conclusion through reflection on his experience when looking at his son's face,

How he looks, when I last saw him, what I know about his personality, his upbringing and education, the sound of his voice, his dry sense of humor, my emotional reactions to him, and so on . . . . To handle this information efficiently, the brain has to symbolize it. This, in a nutshell, is the purpose of qualia. Qualia symbolize a vast repository of tacit and unarticulated data that must be present for a sufficient amount of time. Qualia, the elements of conscious experience, enable the brain to effortlessly manipulate this *simultaneous information.*[27]

Koch's program of research aims to discover the neuronal correlates of qualia. He confesses, however, that even if he knew which neurons must be active, and in precisely what manner, for a given quale to be felt, he still could not fully account for the *feeling* of blueness as he gazes upon a midsummer's sky. This jump, from the physiological activity of nerve cells to the subjective experience of a quale, is what philosophers call the *explanatory gap*, and nobody knows how to get across it.

Evaluation. The experience of consciousness is enough to convince most people that mind is *not just* brain. Still, the challenge for philosophers is to shape a theory that argues persuasively and logically for the impossibility of reducing mind to brain. Donald Davidson's theory of anomalous monism comes close. It is an improvement over basic physicalism because it makes a strong case for the irreducibility of mental properties. However, a couple of issues make it less than ideal. First, its reliance on the rationality of mental states weakens its relevance to mental illness because mental patients often have irrational beliefs and exhibit incomprehensible actions. One hesitates to accept anomalous monism as a valid philosophy of mind if it only applies to some people but not to others. Second, and unfortunately, Davidson's ideas are embedded in heavy logic and academic jargon. As a consequence, ordinary folk will find it difficult to endorse anomalous monism as *their* philosophy of mind. David Chalmers's argument about zombies, by contrast, has an immediate intuitive appeal but is panned by fellow philosophers. I, too, find it difficult to imagine that Chalmers, or anyone else, has an identical twin that lacks consciousness.

Even though I am not fully persuaded by the arguments of Davidson and Chalmers, I am inescapably drawn to their general conclusion, namely, that mind is *not just* brain. Chalk it up to a gut feeling, if you will. One is tempted to endorse the concept of *property dualism,* according to which some things have two types of inherent properties, one mental and one physical. I will have more to say about property dualism below, but for now it is enough to point out that while the concept goes some way in affirming our subjective experience, it does not resolve the philosophical question of whether mental properties can be reduced to physical properties. Reduction is a delicate issue, and it will probably remain so for a long time.

As for the explanatory gap between phenomenal experience and neuronal facts, I believe that it will not so much close, as disappear. The history of ideas about gravity provides a good example of what is likely to happen. People used to wonder why things fall to the ground; it was a mystery. Aristotle wrote that heavy objects fall because they *belong* in the center of the world, which was to say, in the center of the earth. Later, Galileo and others quantified the rates at which objects fall as functions of their weights. This work eventually culminated in Newton's Universal Law of Gravity, which had the added value of incorporating in a single principle not only falling objects but also the attractive force that acts on any pair of objects. Finally, with Einstein's theory of General Relativity, gravity was swallowed up by a grand conception that unites matter, space, and time. Today, following on a history of careful observations, proven predictions, and elaborate theories, we no longer worry about gravity. We do not debate either its essence or its mechanism. Only children and ingenuous adults occasionally ponder whether science has *really* explained why objects fall to the ground. In a similar manner, I suspect that the accumulated mass of neuroscientific knowledge will eventually lead us to stop worrying about how the brain generates consciousness.

Can Mental Phenomena Cause Anything?

Perhaps the issue most relevant to mental illness is that of mental causation. We all have the sense that we can make things happen by just exercising our minds. We can move our limbs "at will," we can change our thoughts, and we can change our plans. Does this mean that we can cause enough disruption in our minds that we can create mental illness? What exactly does it mean to say that mental stress, psychological confusion, or dangerous ideas cause mental illness? And conversely, can mental work undo mental illness?

Let us consider a mundane example of possible mental causation. Imagine that you feel thirsty, and you get up to take a drink from the refrigerator. What is the true cause of your leg movements as you move to the kitchen? Is it the firing of action potentials in the neurons of your brain, or is it your desire to drink? This is the problem of mental causation. It lies at the heart of the mind–body problem.[28]

The contemporary advocates of mental causation shun René Descartes' assumption that mind exists as a substance, but they share his conviction that human actions are not fully explained by physiological events alone. They are *property dualists*. Property dualism is the belief that phenomena like desires, thoughts, and plans, have both mental properties and physical properties. Some property dualists say that mental states can be reduced to physical states in the brain (implying supervenience), whereas other property dualists say that mental properties cannot be reduced. Despite the difference of opinion regarding reduction, most property dualists believe in mental causation.

In their excellent discussion of mental causation, Robb and Heil use an analogy to facilitate thinking about how an object's mental properties can cause physical effects.[29] They ask us to imagine a paperweight with certain *physical properties* relating to its chemical composition. In addition, we can speak of the paperweight's shape, size, and weight; these additional properties are analogous to *mental properties*. When the paperweight is dropped into soft clay, it forms a depression with measurable dimensions. What causes the specific characteristics of the depression? If you say that the width, length, and depth of the depression depend on the shape, size, and weight of the paperweight, then you are answering as would a property dualist. Now think again about moving to the kitchen for a drink. Property dualists say that thirst, like the paperweight, has two types of properties: physical properties, because thirst is realized in the brain, and mental properties because thirst is something of which we are conscious (or of which we can become conscious). They maintain that it is the mental property of thirst that causes us to go to the kitchen.

Not everyone is convinced of mental causation. Both skeptics and outright opponents point to the *exclusion principle*, which states that every event in the physical world must have a physical cause.[30] This is a fundamental premise of science, and it is accepted by most people. A related premise states that whenever a sufficient physical cause is known, no additional cause should be considered because it would be irrelevant. This, too, is reasonable. From these two premises, it follows that if a physical event has a known physical cause (and most do), any proposed mental cause must be excluded. Because human behaviors are physical events for which causes can be found in the nervous system, it is wrong to imagine mental or psychological causes of behaviors. The exclusion argument is simple and compelling. One of its strengths is that it can be successfully employed to deny mental causation under every one of the major theories in contemporary philosophy of mind. Anomalous monism is particularly vulnerable because it denies the existence of laws governing the relationship between mental events and physical events. As with the issue of reduction, the property dualists are split on the issue of mental causation. Some believe in it while others say that only the physical properties of events can cause things to happen.

One is led to think, therefore, that mental causation may simply be illusory. If so, what is the use of mental properties? Are they good for anything? The answer may well be *no*, mental properties are *useless*, they are *epiphenomenal*. As explained earlier in this chapter, epiphenomena are inconsequential by-products. An epiphenomenal event is something real, but it is ineffectual in causing anything to happen. Jaegwon Kim makes a strong case for declaring qualia epiphenomenal. I mentioned his belief that qualia cannot be reduced. Therefore, since only physical objects and physical properties can be causes (from the exclusion principle), no quale can ever be a cause. "A physicalist," says Kim, "who embraces a position like this must accept epiphenomenalism for the physically irreducible mental residue."[31] On the other hand, Kim maintains that all *intentional* mental phenomena, including beliefs, desires, decisions, etc., can be reduced and, therefore, can be causes.

Evaluation. I am inclined to side with Jaegwon Kim on the issue of causation. Intentions (in the broad, philosophical sense) cause things to happen, but only *by virtue of* the brain events that represent (realize) the intentional state. Feelings and qualia, by contrast, are simply epiphenomena so they cannot cause anything to happen. Epiphenomenalism is a mouthful and it smells bad, but it is real and not anything to be afraid of. Evolution has produced many epiphenomena, for example, the red color of our blood and illusory visual effects. I see nothing wrong with things that have no reason, no purpose, no usefulness—but just are.

Summary and Forward Glance

Certain problems in the philosophy of mind are not easily resolved. Indeed, some of the so-called problems may well be mysteries that will never find solutions. And yet, there is movement, some would say progress. Notably, learned opinion has shifted away from theories that take mind to be an independent substance, as championed by Descartes and Aquinas, and towards theories that assume some form of physicalism. Most, but not all, contemporary philosophers accept that our mental lives are the products of our brains, and everything mental is dependent on something physical. In my opinion as well, physicalism is the best philosophy of mind.

While physicalism has its share of philosophical complexities, its main virtue is the simplifying monistic principle that only physical things exist. In accepting physicalism, therefore, we recognize the absurdity of positing a disease in something that does not actually exist. Thus, the preponderance of modern philosophical thought is inconsistent with the literal interpretation of mental illness as a disease of the mind.

Property dualism is a version of physicalism, and thus a form of monism, because it insists that only properties have dual natures; the thing itself is always made of matter. I believe that property dualism is valid for intentions, feelings, desires, qualia, opinions, and everything else that we would want to call mental. Whether or not all mental properties can be reduced to physical properties is a particularly difficult question that has driven philosophers to invent clever arguments on all sides. Unfortunately, it is difficult to convey the full flavor of those arguments here. Suffice it to say, I agree with Kim who thinks that the *intentional* aspects of mind, that is, those thoughts and feelings that are *about something*, can be reduced, whereas feelings and qualia cannot be reduced.

My conclusions here consolidate those of the previous chapters, namely that substance dualism is the wrong way to begin thinking about mental illness. Mental illness is not in the mind. Once we decide in favor of a physicalist philosophy, the task of understanding mental illness is simplified because we can focus on biological causes and ignore intangible, imaginary causes. In the next chapter, I will review the science of mental illness. My main point will be that defects in the normal program for growing the brain lead to chemical and anatomical abnormalities which, in turn, cause the symptoms of mental illness. The science in the next chapter is fully reductive in the explanatory and methodological senses. Nevertheless, not all explanations of mental illness need to be reductive, so in the final chapter I will return to philosophy in order to justify certain other types of explanations.

Notes

1.   The figure comes from a search of Current Contents using the Ovid database.
2.   McLaughlin et al., 2009, p. 3.
3.   Kim, 2005, pp. 30–31.
4.   Skinner, 1971.
5.   Ryle, 1949.
6.   Churchland, 1986.
7.   Crick, 1994; Koch, 2004.
8.   Cooper, 2007, p. 106.
9.   Here the terminology becomes confusing. The original version of physicalism is known as the identity theory, but later it also became known as "type physicalism" to distinguish it from "token physicalism," the revised version of physicalism. To simplify, I will henceforth speak only of the original version and the revised version.
10. Fodor, 1981.
11. Van Gulick, 2009, p. 149.
12. Ibid., p. 145.
13. Dennett, 1991, pp. 369–411.
14. Chalmers, 1996, pp. 293–94.
15. See the exchange between Chalmers and John Searle in Chalmers, 1997.
16. Fodor, 1981, p. 119.
17. Cooper, 2007, pp. 109–10.
18. Ibid., pp. 102–03.
19. Davidson, 1980; for a full treatment of Davidson's philosophy of mind, see Yoo, 2009.
20. Cooper, 2007, pp. 114–17.
21. Ibid., p. 115.
22. Chalmers, 1996, pp. 94–5.
23. Searle, 1997.
24. See Dennett, 1991, pp. 281–82; 309–14.
25. For example, Kim, 2005, p. 24.
26. Kim, 2009, p. 42.
27. Koch, 2004, p. 242.
28. In addition to the other references cited in this section, see Bennett, 2007, for further discussion.
29. Robb, D. and J. Heil. Mental Causation, *The Stanford Encyclopedia of Philosophy* (Summer 2009), E.N. Zalta (ed.), http://plato.stanford.edu/archives/sum2009/entries/mental-causation/.
30. Kim, 2005, 2009.
31. Kim, 2009, p. 42.

6

Mental Illnesses are Brain Illnesses

I have suggested that Cartesian dualism provides a poor platform for understanding mind and mental illness. Moreover, dualism throws obstacles in the way of scientific investigation because it beckons us to consider immaterial mechanisms and nonexistent entities. By rejecting metaphysical dualism in favor of physicalism, modern neuroscience has advanced to the stage where we now have a pretty good idea about the causes and biological manifestations of mental illness.

In this chapter, I will describe how the human brain develops from the embryo onward, how it works, and why it sometimes fails to function as it should. Although the brain is highly complex, the essentials of its operation can be described with a minimum of technical language. The rapid pace of research may prove me wrong about certain judgments and predictions, but no new discoveries can shake my confidence in explanatory and methodological reduction, for I believe that higher level phenomena like mental activity are best understood in terms of lower level phenomena like brain activity. Note, however, that scientific evidence by itself, no matter how compelling it may be, is insufficient *to prove* that mental illness is reducible to brain illness. Ultimately, the acceptability of mind-to-brain reduction depends on one's philosophic convictions.

Biological Psychiatry

Science is concerned with mechanisms. The mechanisms of causation are particularly interesting for medical scientists because they hold the keys to prevention and treatment. Given that mental illness is a disease of the brain, the focus today is on genetics and neuroscience. Genetics was not yet heard of in Descartes' time, of course, but many people, including Descartes, were definitely interested in the brain. After encountering indifference and outright rejection for centuries, Hippocrates's medical model for mental illness had eventually gained traction by the seventeenth century. Europe was seized with an enthusiasm for knowledge about the human body, and Réne Descartes joined in the discussion. In fact, he and William Harvey (1578–1657) were influential in transforming biological curiosity into the search for mechanisms. Descartes' writings make no mention of mental illness, but he did speculate on how the brain works. Apart from promoting the pineal gland as the site of exchanges between the mind and the brain, Descartes proposed a mechanism to account for bodily movements. Refreshing ideas first articulated by Galen in the second century, he supposed that *animal spirits* travel in nerves throughout the brain. Here is his description of this vague motor physiology:

> . . . animal spirits, which resemble a very subtle wind, or rather a flame which is very pure and very vivid, and which, continually rising up in great abundance from the heart to the brain, thence proceeds through the nerves to the muscles, thereby giving the power of motion to all the members.[1]

Descartes believed the spirits to be airy, but nonetheless things of substance, things that could open and close valves in muscles. The significance of animal spirits as functioning physical entities becomes apparent in Nicholas Malebranche's (1638–1715) hypothesis to explain hallucinations, a characteristic symptom of psychotic mental illness. After Hippocrates, this is one of the earliest examples of a biological explanation in the medical model of psychiatry.

> [I]t sometimes happens that persons whose animal spirits are highly agitated by fasting, vigils, a high fever, or some violent passion have the internal fibers of their brain set in motion as forcefully as by external objects. Because of this, such people sense what they should only imagine, and they think they see objects before their eyes which are only in their imaginations.[2]

Finally, with Thomas Willis (1621–75), we get genuine observational research on the human brain. Although Willis was, in his own words, "addicted . . . to the opening of heads," he was not a barbarian.[3] On the contrary, he was an exceptionally bright and curious gentleman who sought to understand the structure and function of the brain. Toward this end, he performed numerous postmortem brain dissections; these allowed him to produce the first accurate descriptions of cerebral nerves and cerebral blood vessels. He was interested in mental disorders, but he found no traces of these conditions in his dissected brains. Nevertheless, in keeping with the times, he ventured to speculate that nerve spirits are the root cause. He thought that the spirits produce tiny controlled explosions in the brain and that the damage caused by these explosions creates mental illness. This original idea, among many others, is contained in his book, *The Soul of Brutes* (1683), which has been described as "the most complete account of a brain-based psychiatry since the Greeks began practicing medicine."[4] In scientific outlook, as well as in anatomical accuracy, Willis set a standard of inquiry that became the foundation for modern developments in biological psychiatry.

Science is a questioning activity; therefore, when scientists investigate mental illness, they frame their goals as questions. Here are the main questions that they seek to answer:

1. What are the *biomarkers*? or, What anatomical, chemical, or physiological abnormalities can be identified in the brains of mentally ill persons?
2. What are the *mechanisms*? or, How do the physical anomalies in the brain explain the mental and behavioral symptoms?
3. What are the *causes*? or, Which events or conditions are responsible for the brain's abnormalities?

The distinction between mechanisms and causes is not absolute, and some people prefer to speak of *proximal causes* and *ultimate causes*. The proximal causes are equivalent to the brain mechanisms that produce the symptoms, while the ultimate causes are those that initially create the brain abnormalities. In practice, research into mental illness proceeds step-by-step, with each individual research project addressing just a single question from the list above. In the bigger picture, however, an answer to one question provides clues to other answers. Genetic studies of mental illness illustrate the linkages. Since genes have specific functions, discovering which gene, or set of genes, is causing the illness helps investigators to find biomarkers and mechanisms. Conversely, finding biomarkers facilitates the search for causes because now one can look for genes that have functions related to the biomarkers.

Although in many respects medicine has come a long way since Hippocrates's time, even the most up-to-date doctors are reluctant to offer definitive explanations for all but a few of the most common diseases. (Hippocrates, you will remember, confidently stated that all diseases are caused by either an excess or a deficiency in one or more of the four humors.) Among the medical conditions that are hardest to explain are cancer, diabetes, high blood pressure, and heart disease. These conditions are generally thought to be caused by multiple factors acting together, with both genetics and the environment contributing. They are known as *complex diseases*. Medical opinion holds that mental illnesses are likewise complex in this sense, as I will explain.

My discussion focuses on schizophrenia, which many people view as the prototypical mental illness. In his book, *Schizophrenia: The Sacred Symbol of Psychiatry*, published in 1976, Thomas Szasz wrote that "[t]here is at present no demonstrable histopathological or pathophysiological evidence to support the claim that schizophrenia is a disease. Indeed, if there were any, the supporters of this claim would be the first to assert that schizophrenia is not a mental disease but a brain disease."[5] If Szasz's statement was a challenge to the biological psychiatrists of the time, thirty-five years later, we can safely say that the scientific investigators have successfully met the challenge, for there is now incontrovertible evidence of pathology in the brains of schizophrenics, and few informed people deny that schizophrenia is indeed a brain disease.

Schizophrenia is both highly debilitating and very prevalent, with about 1 percent of the population affected at any given time. Although the definition of schizophrenia is controversial, certain symptoms are characteristic. The so-called *positive symptoms* are those that are not ordinarily found in healthy individuals; they include hallucinations (usually auditory), delusions (often paranoid), incoherent speech, and disorganized thought. The *negative symptoms* involve normal attributes that are weakened in persons with schizophrenia; they include poverty of thought, reduced emotion (low affect), reduced ambition, and less social interaction. In addition to the positive and negative symptoms, there are more subtle cognitive effects, including the inability to focus attention, a reduced short-term memory, and deficits in the so-called executive functions of planning, action initiation, and the selection of relevant sensory cues.

Current science supports a broad but widely accepted hypothesis for the genesis of schizophrenia.[6] I will outline that hypothesis now and then describe its scientific justification in the remainder of the chapter. Most authorities believe that schizophrenia begins long before the first appearance of its symptoms. A genetic predisposition causes some people to be especially vulnerable to certain environments (biological, physical, or social) that affect the normal development of the brain. The first critical events most likely occur in the second or third trimester of pregnancy, or at the time of birthing. As a result, the neural circuitry of the brain is altered. These alterations affect the brain's functions, but the cognitive and behavioral abnormalities characteristic of psychosis emerge only in late adolescence or early adulthood, after the brain has undergone further development. Changes in hormonal functions and social relationships during adolescence bring additional stresses, which trigger expression of the disease at this stage in life.

Schizophrenia is probably not a single disease, but rather the name for a group of disorders with related symptoms. Cancer, even that which we call "breast cancer," is also not a single disease. A number of different genetic mutations produce a variety of breast cancers, each of which differs in respect to the location, appearance, and progression of the disorder. In the case of schizophrenia, the distinction between related conditions is currently based on behavioral and psychological criteria, which are inherently imprecise and often ambiguous. Biological markers, including genetics, are just beginning to be useful for distinguishing schizophrenia subtypes. However, owing to the absence of fully objective and reliable criteria, and despite the inaccuracy of referring to schizophrenia as if it were unitary, I will not distinguish among the family of schizophrenic disorders in the account that follows.

Biomarkers

Biomarkers are physical markers, usually in the brain or in the body fluids, that appear in patients but not in normal individuals, or at least appear more commonly in patients than in normal individuals. They can be useful for detecting and diagnosing diseases and potentially critical for developing therapies. It is important to understand, however, that the discovery of a biomarker does not necessarily imply the discovery of a cause of the disease. Investigators must rule out biomarkers that result from medications taken by the patients or from the patients' lifestyles. In the case of schizophrenia, the diseased state is typically associated with reduced physical activity, smoking, and dietary irregularities. Medications and lifestyles can affect brain chemistry in ways that correlate with the illness, but do not constitute causes of the disease.

The early attempts to find biomarkers for schizophrenia were disappointing. In central Europe, in the late nineteenth century, medical scientists launched a major effort inspired by the introduction of high-quality microscopes and improved methods for staining tissues. However, they found nothing that distinguished the brains of the mentally ill from those of normal persons. Later, after a period in which psychoanalysis dominated the field of psychiatry, a second period of biological psychiatry emerged in the 1960s. This time, poor judgments and premature publications led to false hopes. Various reports called attention to "pink spots" in the urine (from a metabolite of compounds related to epinephrine), high concentrations of serum creatine phosphokinase (an enzyme), and traces of an unusual protein (taraxein). Sadly, after the enthusiasm that greeted the announcement of each new marker, disappointment ensued when the initial results could not be replicated.

Despite the early failures, recent years have seen reports of several valid biomarkers for mental illnesses, thanks to greatly improved research methods and an invigorated system of peer review that screens out dubious claims.[7] As one might expect, the biomarkers for schizophrenia are found predominately in those areas of the brain that support the functions that are disrupted in the disease, that is, attention and planning (prefrontal cortex and hippocampus), language (temporal cortex), and audition (dorsal thalamus). In the following paragraphs, I will highlight the most reliable physical and chemical markers for schizophrenia; some will be described in greater detail later in the chapter.

From imaging studies of living brains, two robust biomarkers have been identified. One concerns the size of the ventricles, or the fluid-filled spaces of the brain. Numerous reports find that the ventricles are larger in persons affected by schizophrenia than in normal individuals. The second important finding is that the cerebral cortex, the brain's outer shell, is thinner in schizophrenia brains than in normal brains. A plausible interpretation linking these two cardinal findings is that the reduced cortical volume allows an expansion of the ventricles.

Other biomarkers for schizophrenia were discovered through detailed, quantitative analyses of postmortem brain samples. For example, in the prefrontal cortex and the hippocampus, certain types of *neurons* (nerve cells) are smaller in schizophrenia brains than in normal brains. One type of neuron is consistently found in locations that are slightly displaced from the normal locations. As well, neurotransmitters are significantly affected, with biomarkers reported for every one of the major systems, namely acetylcholine, serotonin, glutamate, dopamine, and gamma-aminobutyric acid (GABA). Each system appears to be affected in multiple ways, typically involving the production, receptor binding, and metabolism of the transmitter substance. From studies of postmortem brains, investigators can also determine patterns of gene expression, that is, they can measure the levels of protein production at the time of death.[8] Dozens of genes have been identified whose activity, in the aforementioned brain regions, is significantly altered in schizophrenia brains compared to normal brains. These genes code for proteins that cluster around energy metabolism, calcium homeostasis, neurotransmission, and immune functions. Interestingly, one type of pathology that is *not* ordinarily found in association with schizophrenia is degeneration. Quantitative counts show that the number of neurons in schizophrenia brains is no different (on average) from the number in normal brains.

Although biomarkers have great potential as tools in research and clinical practice, they must be carefully interpreted. The observed differences in cortical thickness and ventricular volume are especially valuable because they appear either prior to, or at the same time as, the behavioral symptoms, and before the use of any medications. Therefore, they are unlikely to be caused by the medications rather than the disease. The numerous reports of dysfunction in multiple neurotransmitter systems, on the other hand, raise concern. Further research is needed to determine whether all of the observed alternations are primary causes of schizophrenia, or whether some might represent incidental, correlated effects.

In order for a biomarker to be maximally useful, it must be reliably associated with one particular disease, for example, schizophrenia, but not with any other disease, for example, bipolar disorder. Unfortunately, it can be difficult to determine who has schizophrenia, who does not, and who has one of several related diseases. This is a problem that affects not only the interpretation of biomarkers but also other aspects of research and clinical practice. In North America, researchers and clinicians diagnose all psychiatric disorders by following guidelines contained in the *Diagnostic and Statistical Manual of Mental Disorders, fourth edition*, commonly known as DSM-IV.[9] For schizophrenia, the diagnosis rests on a doctor's judgment that the person displays two or more symptoms from a list of seven (including both positive and negative symptoms as defined above), *and* that he or she behaves abnormally in social situations. Thus, the diagnosis of psychiatric disorders relies on *subjective, qualitative* criteria, while the identification of biomarkers uses *objective, quantitative* criteria, and therein lies the problem.

The subjective nature of the diagnoses based on DSM-IV criteria undoubtedly leads to errors because, on the one hand, some people who are actually ill are not identified as such, while, on the other hand, some basically healthy people are incorrectly diagnosed with schizophrenia. Borderline cases characterized by very mild symptoms are difficult to diagnose and especially subject to errors because the diagnosis must be all-or-none. The psychiatrist must declare either that the person has the disease or that he/she does not have the disease; she cannot conclude that the patient is just-barely, not-quite normal. Moreover, the DSM-IV criteria allow two individuals with different symptoms to both be diagnosed with schizophrenia. For example, one person may have only hallucinations (a positive symptom) and low energy (a negative symptom), while another person may have only incoherent speech (a positive symptom) and low emotions (a negative symptom). While both individuals have sets of symptoms that satisfy the DSM-IV criteria for schizophrenia, in reality the symptoms are quite dissimilar, and the two individuals may actually suffer from different diseases. The distinction, in such cases, between one disease and two diseases can be critical for interpreting biomarkers because if both individuals have the same disease, they should have the same biomarkers, whereas if they have different diseases, they should have different biomarkers. Errors in diagnosis, therefore, can confound the statistical association between a biomarker and the supposedly single disease, schizophrenia.

Many leading psychiatrists would like the forthcoming revised version of the DSM, DSM-V, to include objective criteria for diagnoses. Biomarkers could serve this role, provided that they are unaffected by drug effects and lifestyles and they are specific for schizophrenia. At present, cortical thickness and ventricle volume satisfy the first requirement, but not the second. I am confident, however, that we will eventually be able to test for schizophrenia and other psychiatric disorders using reliable, objective measures. In principle, it should not be different from testing for diabetes by measuring blood glucose levels.

Mechanisms

For some people, the brain is simply the most complex organ in the human body, others say it is the most complex thing known to human civilization, while still others boldly proclaim that the brain is the most complex structure in the entire universe. Whatever the exact formulation, there is no doubt that the brain is very complex, and this fact is important for understanding the physical aspect of schizophrenia. The complexity of the brain lies mostly in extremely small structures, and the compactness creates severe technical difficulties for investigators. Even with valid biomarkers in hand, scientists are challenged to understand how an anatomical or physiological abnormality creates the symptoms of schizophrenia or any other psychiatric illness. To see why this is so, one needs to know some facts about the brain's structure and physiology. If at times you question why it is necessary that I provide so much detail, it is because only the details allow one to understand the brain in health and mental illness. It is the amazing, beautiful complexity of the brain that makes it so vulnerable to disease.

The business of the brain is to process information. The information is present in the form of electrical currents that flow across the membranes of nerve cells. When information is conveyed from one neuron to another, it must travel across minutely small gaps, called *synapses*, that separate the membranes of adjacent neurons. Scientists discovered, in the middle of the twentieth century, that information usually travels across synapses not by electricity but by small molecules, called *neurotransmitters*. The pattern of synaptic connections between neurons is remarkably constant from brain to brain. Equally remarkable is the fact that neuroscientists can describe these patterns in great detail.

Figure 6.1 illustrates some of the known differences between normal brains and schizophrenic brains. In other words, it shows reliable biomarkers. The figure depicts a small sample of neurons and synaptic connections in the prefrontal lobe of the cerebral cortex. This region of the brain is of particular interest because it is associated with many of the cognitive functions affected by schizophrenia and it is the last area of the cortex to mature.[10] I emphasize that Figure 6.1 is a gross simplification. For example, the figure illustrates two types of neurons: the black triangles represent the so-called *pyramidal neurons* that excite other neurons through synapses (shown as lines ending in small open triangles); the black circles represent smaller *inhibitory neurons* that suppress the electrical activity of other neurons (lines ending in small black circles). In reality, each of these two neuronal types—the pyramidal neurons and the inhibitory neurons—is represented by five or more clearly distinguishable *subtypes*. Also, the number of neurons is grossly underrepresented in the figure. In reality, the prefrontal lobe of the human brain contains about 50,000 neurons in each cubic millimeter.[11] To appreciate how densely packed are these neurons and how small they are, consider a column of cells extending down from the top of the cortex to the bottom (a distance of about 2.5 millimeters). If the column had a diameter equal to the width of *this dot*: ·, the column would contain about 40,000 neurons. This same small volume of tissue would contain about 300 million synapses! Each synapse is about twenty *nano*meters across, making it invisible except by electron microscopy. These numbers give some sense of the enormous complexity of the cerebral cortex.

In schizophrenia, the cell bodies of the pyramidal neurons in the upper part of the prefrontal cortex are smaller and have shorter branches (dendrites) than in normal brains (no. 1 in Figure 6.1), so they receive fewer messages from other neurons. In addition, two specific types of inhibitory connections are weakened in schizophrenia (at locations 2, 3, and 5; see the figure legend for details). Lastly, the entire cortical tissue is slightly shrunken in schizophrenia (no. 4).

It is natural to ask, having identified these anatomical biomarkers, how they explain schizophrenia. How do they account for the behaviors and mental aberrations that characterize the disease? Unfortunately, there is no clear answer to this question at the present time. It is unlikely, however, that they have no effect, so one is entitled to speculate. It is possible that the anatomical changes cause some neurons in the schizophrenia brain to become more active than normal or, conversely, less active. These physiological effects would exaggerate, diminish, or even silence certain neural messages.

I suspect, however, that the anatomical changes affect not so much the amount of neural activity as the timing of the activity. The principal type of electrical signal that neurons use to encode information is the *action potential*. A single action potential consists of a brief, explosive current that lasts only a few *milli*seconds, hence the expression, neurons *fire* action potentials. The exact timing of successive action potentials is so crucial for information processing that even a fraction of a millisecond can make or break a message. Therefore,

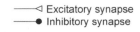

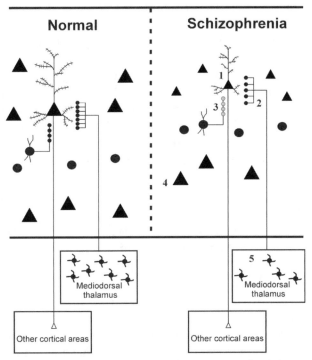

Triangles and circles represent pyramidal neurons and inhibitory neurons, respectively. The depth of the cortex, shown here between the thick horizontal lines, is about 2.5 millimeters. The numbers indicate the well-established differences between schizophrenia brains and normal brains, as described below:

1. Smaller cells in the upper parts of the cortex.

2. Fewer inhibitory synapses formed by axons coming from the mediodorsal thalamus.

3. Lower concentrations of the neurotransmitter GABA in terminals of inhibitory neurons.

4. Reduced thickness of the cortex (mostly due to a thinning near the top).

5. Fewer neurons in the mediodorsal thalamus.

Source: Figure adapted from Harrison, 1999; Frankle et al., 2003.

Figure 6.1 Schematic summary of anatomical biomarkers for schizophrenia in the prefrontal cortex

if the pyramidal neurons in the right-hand portion of Figure 6.1 are a tiny bit early in firing their action potentials, or a tiny bit late, they may convey misleading or confusing signals to the neurons on the receiving end of the messages. (See boxes labeled "other cortical areas.") Some evidence for an impairment of this type has recently been reported.[12] The investigation studied the brains of mice that were genetically engineered to carry one of the risk factors for schizophrenia (a microdeletion of human chromosome 22). In normal mice that are engaged in the performance of a simple memory task, the electrical activity in both the prefrontal lobe and the hippocampus is rhythmical, that is, the activity is temporally patterned with regularly spaced peaks and troughs. Furthermore, and importantly, anatomical connections ensure that the peaks and troughs of activity are synchronized across the two structures. The synchrony is greatly reduced, however, in the mice that carry the genetic alteration, and the reduced synchrony correlates with poorer behavioral performance on the memory task. In humans, the prefrontal cortex is responsible for executive functions, so if there is a similar disruption of synchrony in humans, it could create delusions, incoherent speech, or other symptoms of schizophrenia.

With the discussion above, I have tried to convey a sense of brain function at the level of its cellular organization, which is to say I have stressed the brain's *microcircuitry*. I believe that it is extremely important to understand this level of organization. People with no formal schooling in neuroscience tend to learn about the brain through media reports that rarely, if ever, discuss microcircuitry. Television, newsprint, and the Web all prefer to report neuroscience news based on whole brain imaging methods such as functional magnetic resonance imaging (fMRI). A typical news item will show brain area X "lighting up" when a subject or patient performs task Y, thus implying that brain area X is responsible for task Y. Sadly, these stories often convey a misleading picture of how the brain works. Niko Logothetis, an authority on brain imaging methods, has written about the limitations of fMRI.[13] First, it yields ambiguous information about the physiological status of neurons, and second, it is incapable of detecting the activities of individual neurons or small groups of neurons functioning in microcircuits. The latter point is especially pertinent. Because schizophrenia probably alters activity at the microcircuit level of neural organization, the fMRI method does not have enough resolving power to be useful for investigating schizophrenia. Indeed, fMRI has contributed little to the understanding of schizophrenia.[14]

Causes: Neural Development

How to build a body, how to build a brain? Experts describe the construction of the human brain as a "feat of unimaginable intricacy" because it requires huge numbers of cells to be connected (via synapses) in just the right way.[15] Since most of the brain's development is complete by the time a baby is born, my focus will be on the major events that occur in the nine months from fertilization to birth.[16] Once again, the message will be in the details. Given the complexity of the brain, it is hardly surprising that errors sometimes occur during its development. Still more remarkably, most of the time things turn out just fine.

We begin with the production of about 100 billion nerve cells, along with 5–10 times as many support cells, called glia cells. These new cells are created by cell divisions, with the exact timing of each division controlled by two types of molecules, the cyclins and the kinases. Throughout most of the prenatal period, approximately 50,000 new cells are created every second. All newly born neurons must accomplish two big tasks: first, position themselves in their proper places; and second, make connections with other cells that will either receive their messages or send messages to them. Special challenges are faced by those neurons that are fated to go to the cerebral cortex because here, in the fully developed brain, specific cell types lie at specific depths from the surface (see Figure 6.1). The difference between a correct placement and an incorrect placement can be as small as fifty *micro*meters. The neurons are born at the base of the cortex, and from there they migrate upward by clinging to long strands of glia cell fibers. The first-born neurons take up positions in the deep cortical layers, whereas the later-born neurons migrate past the early ones to take positions in the upper layers. Migrating neurons are guided to their predetermined, correct locations by molecules that are released from cells lying near the surface of the cortex. Because the concentration of these molecules is high near the top and low near the bottom, migrating neurons can hone in on their target positions by "reading" the concentrations as they move along. Interestingly, secretions of one of the main guidance molecules, reelin, are 30–60 percent reduced in schizophrenia brains compared to normal brains. Investigators think that an insufficiency of reelin may explain why certain types of neurons are misplaced in schizophrenia and why the microcircuitry of schizophrenia brains is aberrant.[17] Two other molecules, named disrupted-in-schizophrenia 1 (DISC1) and neuregulin-1 (NRG1), are broadly involved in both the early initial production of neurons and their subsequent migrations. Like reelin, DISC1 and NRG1 are implicated in schizophrenia through genetic and biochemical studies.

Once in position, the young neurons begin to grow long fibers, or *axons*, that reach out to contact other neurons. Depending on which neurons must be contacted, the axons can extend anywhere from a few tens of *micro*meters to roughly one-half meter. Small groups of pioneer fibers go out first, navigating their way in a relatively barren environment to their predetermined destinations. Later, the remaining axons follow the paths laid down by the pioneers. Just as the neuronal cell bodies rely on molecular guidance, so too do the axons use molecular cues to locate their intended targets. Some molecules form concentration gradients in the spaces between tissues of the brain to either attract or repel growing axons. Meanwhile, other chemicals, called *adhesion molecules*, stick out from the surfaces of cells and attach to axons when they approach. The adhesion molecules function like Velcro fabrics, and they come in a great variety of different "textures." Adhesion between an axon and a guidance cell occurs only when the texture of the molecules on the axon matches that of the molecules on the guidance cell; this constraint ensures that the migrating axons follow the correct paths. One particular adhesion molecule, named, appropriately, the neuronal cell adhesion molecule (NCAM), is implicated in schizophrenia. Persons with schizophrenia tend to have mutations in the NCAM gene, reduced brain concentrations of NCAM, and impairment of that portion of the molecule that is responsible for grabbing axons.[18]

Neurons are also required to be of the correct type, and there are hundreds of different types distinguished by their morphologies, chemistries, and synaptic connections. Two examples of neuronal cell types are shown in Figure 6.1. When neurons are first born, they are indistinguishable one from the other; there are no discernable types. Thereafter, they are influenced by molecules both inside the cells and outside in the surrounding fluid as they progressively differentiate. The process is similar to that whereby all the other cell types in the body differentiate. In the case of nerve cells, it requires the participation of more than half of all the genes active in the nervous system. At least one of these genes, named RGS4, is implicated in schizophrenia.

A remarkable feature of development in many regions of the nervous system is that 80 percent of the newly created cells die shortly after they are produced. Massive cell deaths in the embryonic brain are not only normal but likely necessary to eliminate neurons that do not develop into the correct type or that fail to connect with the appropriate set of target neurons. Survival depends on a variety of factors, among which are hormonal signals, activity from synaptic transmission, and most importantly, molecules belonging to the class known as *neurotrophins*, meaning nerve foods. The role of the neurotrophins is to promote the growth and survival of neurons. Rita Levi-Montalcini earned a Nobel Prize for discovering the first neurotrophin, named nerve growth factor. Two other neurotrophins, known as brain-derived neurotrophic factor and neurotophin-3, are of particular interest because mutations in the genes for these molecules are associated with schizophrenia.

And finally, synapses. The importance of synapses cannot be overstated; their correct operation is vital for normal brain function. Incorrect operations at synapses are likely to cause mental disruptions and abnormal behaviors. It is estimated that the adult human brain contains a staggering 1,000 trillion (10^{15}) synapses. On average, each neuron has about 1,000 synapses, sites at which the neuron receives messages from other neurons. The pyramidal cells, shown schematically in Figure 6.1, are unusually rich in synapses, with approximately 10,000 synaptic sites per neuron. Not every synapse represents an input from a different transmitting neuron; often a single transmitting neuron forms multiple synapses with its receiving partner. Nevertheless, each receiving neuron typically listens to messages from about 100 transmitting neurons. Importantly, proper functioning within the nervous system depends on establishing appropriate synaptic connections between specific neuron types in specific brain locations. A large number of different molecules is involved in establishing synapses. Among them is a class of adhesion molecules similar to those mentioned above. One set, comprising proteins in numerous molecular variations, is attached to the tips of the growing axons, while a complementary set of proteins is attached to the potential target cells. The molecules on the axon discriminate the correct targets from the distracting targets by testing for chemical compatibility, and synapses are created only when the molecules on the axon match the molecules on the target cell.

Synapses are formed at a furious pace early in life, only to be eliminated in huge numbers thereafter. In the cerebral cortex, the number of synapses at the end of adolescence is about 65 percent of the number at age 2½. Like the loss of cells, the loss of synapses is a normal process. Neuroscientists see the shedding of cells and synapses as a kind of *neural Darwinism* in which nonoptimal connections are pruned and eliminated. Moreover synapses retain the remarkable ability to reshape connections even after the numbers have stabilized. This so-called *neural plasticity* is enormously important for psychiatry because it is the basis of memory formation. Within their tiny structures, synapses hold a complex biochemical machinery that allows them to respond to real life events. The synapses monitor what a person sees, smells, feels, and hears. Depending on what happens in the person's life and how important it is, individual synapses can either increase or decrease the strength of neural connections. The resulting adjustment to microcircuitry is what creates memories, both conscious and unconscious.[19]

It should come as no surprise that several molecules known to be involved in the processes of synapse formation and neural plasticity are implicated in schizophrenia. Among these are DISC1 and NRG1, which were already mentioned in relation to neuronal production and migration. These molecules, as well as others mentioned in this section, are associated with schizophrenia through genetic studies, to which we now turn.

Causes: Genes

It will be useful to bear in mind a few basic facts as we consider the role that genes play in causing schizophrenia and other mental illnesses. Genes are segments of the molecule deoxyribonucleic acid (DNA). Within each such segment, the sequence of DNA elements, or *nucleotides*, represents the code for a particular protein. The nucleotides are of four types, or "letters," and the specific sequence of letters comprises the code. Every gene lies silent in the cell nucleus until it is put into action by *transcription factors*. When targeted by transcription factors, a gene *expresses*, or makes, a protein. Although they are called "factors," the activating molecules are actually proteins.

Altogether, about one-half of all human genes (c. 20,000 total) are expressed exclusively in the nervous system. Of these, about 8,000 genes are needed just to build the brain and its related structures. Once the system has matured, many of these genes go silent, while others become active and remain active throughout life. I have already named a few of the genes (or their protein products) that have roles in building the nervous system. The transcription factors can now be added to this group of critical genes because transcription factors activate the genes that express the proteins that control development. Transcription factors are responsible for providing the necessary molecular helpers in the right places at the right times. If these events do not occur according to plan, problems inevitably arise, so transcription factors are prime candidates for contributing to psychiatric illnesses. For example, mutations in the gene that codes for the transcription factor zinc finger protein 804A are associated with both schizophrenia and bipolar disorder.

What are gene mutations, and what kinds of problems do they cause? Gene mutations typically involve a change from a nucleotide of one type (a letter) to a nucleotide of a different type. In total, there are about three billion DNA nucleotides organized on twenty-three pairs of human chromosomes. The consequences of a mutation depend on which specific nucleotide (of the four possible ones) is lost and which one replaces it. In some instances, the substitution is neutral, with no change in function. In other cases, protein production is partially or entirely blocked ; conversely, too much protein may be produced. If the mutated gene alters the chemical composition of the protein, its function may be impaired. A mutation can also cause the gene to be expressed in the wrong type of cell. All of these deviations from normal gene function have the potential to impair brain development.

In addition to mutations, many genes occur in variable forms with different nucleotides at specific locations in the different variants. By definition, gene variants are much more common than mutations, and a single variant typically causes little or no effect. However, certain combinations of many variants are potentially problematic.

Numerous studies have shown that heredity (hence, genes) accounts for about 80 percent of the risk for getting schizophrenia. In the early days of medical genetics, researchers anticipated that they would find one, or maybe two, rare mutations causing each psychiatric disease. Unfortunately, this turned out not to be the case. Rather, what has been found is that numerous common variants are associated with each of the major diseases. The most common route to finding these variants is to conduct a *genome-wide association study*. The basic design of these research projects is quite simple. The investigators examine genes in disease-affected individuals and in disease-free individuals. The screening method probes nearly all of the common gene variants (but none of the rare mutations). If a variant appears in significantly more of the disease-affected cases than in the disease-free cases, that variant is said to be associated with the disease, and it becomes a candidate cause of the disease. This type of research is difficult, not just because of technical issues but also because of a problem related to disease diagnosis. Since the DSM-IV relies on subjective criteria, as I explained above, the diagnoses are seldom certain. Consequently, whenever a true case of schizophrenia goes unrecognized or another illness is incorrectly diagnosed as schizophrenia, the statistical association between schizophrenia and a candidate genetic marker is diluted. This can produce misleading or inconclusive results.

With respect to schizophrenia, the genome-wide association studies had identified at least forty-three so-called *susceptibility genes* by the year 2010.[20] Each one is a particular variant form of a common gene. New susceptibility genes continue to be reported, but not every study finds the same genes. Here is a sampling of the most frequently cited susceptibility genes together with their presumed functions; some of the genes were mentioned above:

> Neuregulin 1 (NRG1): Development of inhibitory circuits in the cerebral cortex.
>
> Disrupted-in-schizophrenia 1 (DISC1): Neuronal production and migration; cell-to-cell adhesion.
>
> Dysbindin (DTNBP1): Formation and function of synapses.
>
> Catechol-O-methyl transferase (COMT): Metabolism of dopamine, norepinephrine, and other neurotransmitters.
>
> Neurogranin (NRGN): Memory storage at synapses.
>
> Zinc finger protein 804A (ZNF804A): Transcription factor (activates genes).
>
> Major histocompatability complex (many distinct genes): Immunity.

Although investigators are pleased to have found susceptibility genes, they are not so happy with the low predictive values of the identified genes. That is to say, none is present in anything like every case of schizophrenia, and many are common in disease-free persons. In fact, having one or another of the identified variants only increases by about 10 percent one's chance of getting the disease, and even combining all the susceptibility genes accounts for only a small fraction of the 80 percent heritability. As the disappointment of these results sunk in, geneticists wrote about "the case of the missing heritability," and they characterized the inferred, but unknown genes, as the genome's "dark matter." When investigators reported similar results for autism and bipolar disorder as for schizophrenia, it became clear that fresh ideas were needed to fully explain the inheritance of mental illnesses. Geneticists are currently working on three hypotheses. As I explain each hypothesis below, I will again take schizophrenia as the principal example.

The first hypothesis simply extends the assumptions underlying the genome-wide association studies to include many more susceptibility genes. Instead of expecting a dozen or so genes to associate with risk, current evidence suggests that the risk may arise from "thousands of common [variants] of very small effect."[21] It is possible, too, that different combinations of gene variants drawn from a large pool of risk genes could produce similar behavioral or psychological effects. The prospect of discovering all the influential variants, each with just a "very small" effect, is daunting because the smaller the effect, the larger is the sample size required to detect it. To appreciate the importance of this statistical obstacle, we can look at the genetic contribution to human height differences, which provides an instructive example.

If one measures heights in any large adult population, a continuous range of variation from very short to very tall will be revealed; it will *not* be found that people are either short or tall. This result demonstrates that height, like schizophrenia, is a *polygenetic* or *complex* trait, meaning that it is governed by multiple genes. Polygenetic traits vary quantitatively from one individual to another, whereas monogenetic traits vary qualitatively. The telltale sign suggesting that schizophrenia is also a polygenetic trait is the fact that the positive symptoms (hallucinations, incoherent speech, disorganized thought) vary considerably from mild to severe, depending on the individual. Coincidentally, the heritability of human height differences is about 80 percent heritable, or roughly equal to that of schizophrenia. A study published in 2010 marshaled DNA data from nearly 185,000 adults to discover 180 genes[22] that affect height.[23] However, the combined influence of all 180 genes accounted for only about 10 percent of the variation in height that can be explained by heredity. The authors estimated that another 517 genes may make similar contributions which, when combined with the 180 genes already identified, would still only account for about 16 percent of the variation in height that can be explained by heredity. Notably, to identify these additional genes would require analyzing genes in another 500,000 individuals. These numbers clearly show that to discover genes of very small effect requires samples of very large numbers. It is expensive to conduct such investigations and, for schizophrenia research, there is a natural limit to sample sizes owing to the relatively low prevalence of the disease (about 7 per 1,000 persons). Add to this the inaccessibility of many patients and the need for informed consent, and the difficulty of obtaining a sufficiently large sample becomes apparent. In short, if schizophrenia is indeed caused by a very large number of weakly influential genes, it will not be easy to identify those genes, at least not with the methods currently available.

The second hypothesis takes the opposite approach. Some authorities believe that the risk of schizophrenia comes from a group of rare but very potent mutations.[24] As in the scenario discussed above, different mutations might be responsible in different cases. The idea of rare but potent mutations fits well with our knowledge of the complex molecular cascades that underlie brain development because a single problem occurring anywhere in the normal sequence of molecular events will have deleterious effects on the final outcome. The problem could appear while neuronal cell types are being created, while neurons are migrating, or while synapses are forming. The rare mutations that are invoked by this hypothesis would most likely involve single nucleotides (see note 22). Unfortunately, the probes that are currently used to study gene variants, for example, in gene association studies, are not suitable for detecting single nucleotide variants. The only way to do this is by reading every single letter of the genetic code using a technique known as DNA sequencing. Currently, selected regions of the genome can be sequenced relatively easily, depending on the size of the region, but to discover rare mutations that may lurk in any part of the genome requires that the entire genome be sequenced, covering all three billion nucleotides. This feat was first accomplished in 2001, thanks to a huge effort by many dedicated researchers and funding in the millions of dollars. In the years that followed, the efficiency of whole-genome sequencing has increased dramatically, so much so that an individual's entire genome can now be sequenced in about four days for about $15,000. Most authorities envisage a time in the near future when the cost will be less than $1,000 per genome. Steadily, as the cost drops, it becomes more and more feasible to screen mental patients for rare, but potent, mutations.

A third hypothesis to explain the missing heritability of schizophrenia supposes that researchers have been looking for the wrong type of genetic alteration. So far, we have talked about mutations and variations in the genetic code. Another type of alteration involves the gain or loss of large chunks of DNA; it is called *copy number variation.* Normally, DNA is present in exactly two copies per cell. Occasionally, however, an error occurs during the normal process of DNA replication which results in either the deletion or the duplication of DNA. As few as several hundred DNA letters may be affected, or as many as several million. When DNA is duplicated, proteins may be *over* produced, whereas when DNA is deleted, protein may be *under* produced. Some studies report evidence for an association between copy-number variations and schizophrenia.[25]

Causes: Environment

As mentioned, the heritability of both height and schizophrenia is about 80 percent, which means that the remaining 20 percent is assigned to the environment, and when geneticists speak of *the environment*, they refer not only to animals, plants, and "nature," but to everything to which an individual is exposed in his or her lifetime. Even though a boy may have the genes that would make him six feet tall, he might not grow to more than five feet if his childhood diet lacks certain key nutrients. Likewise, while genetics contributes a large portion of the risk for schizophrenia, it alone cannot account for who gets the disease. Studies of identical twins are very instructive here because both twins have exactly the same genes. Interestingly, even if one twin gets schizophrenia, the chances that other twin will also get schizophrenia are only about 50 percent.[26] Because the correlation is less than 100 percent, factors other than genetics are obviously involved, and yet, twins raised together in the same home experience very similar environments. This leads one to conclude that the critical experiences that trigger schizophrenia are subtle and difficult to detect. One possibility, discussed below, is that the key events occur prior to, or during, birth.

The current idea among leading researchers is that schizophrenia results from the combined effects of a genetic predisposition and environmental stress. From the Greek word, *diathesis,* for disposition, comes the *diathesis-stressor theory,* but the label is more associated with a general framework for ideas than with a full-blown theory. The main idea is that schizophrenia will appear whenever the sum of all genetic and environmental liabilities exceeds a certain threshold level. Accordingly, a person with a strong genetic predisposition will need only a moderate amount of stress to trigger the disease, whereas someone with only a mild genetic predisposition may still get schizophrenia if he or she is subjected to intense stress. Professor

119

Irving I. Gottesman, a leading researcher in the field of psychiatric genetics, gives an example in his excellent book, *Schizophrenia Genesis*.[27] He explains the important but limited role of genes by describing the medical condition favism, which is an anemia that occurs among Mediterranean Greeks and Italians who carry a particular mutant gene. None of the carriers shows any sign of the illness unless they eat fava beans or become exposed to pollen from the bean plants, at which point the anemia begins. In other words, both the gene and the bean are necessary for favism, just as both genes and stress are necessary for schizophrenia. Although the genetics of schizophrenia is more complex than that of favism, the same principle of diathesis plus stressor applies. Gottesman sums up the situation,

> Each kind of relative, in the individual case, has a wide range of possibilities in a complex game of gene-environment Russian roulette; only the averages behave predictably. The combined liability can be modified by many factors, it can be suppressed completely from expressing itself as schizophrenia, or it can be made much worse. That is the essence of the diathesis-stressor formulation—Nature proposes and Nurture disposes.[28]

What, then, are the stressful environments that can trigger schizophrenia? The history of proposed stressors makes for interesting reading because there have been many ideas. Initially, the obvious candidates included life-threatening experiences such as war combat, and ego-shattering experiences such as parental divorce, but neither of these stressors was found to increase the risk of schizophrenia. Psychological and social factors have also received much attention. However, while psychiatrists understand that family relationships and social environments can be stressful, they remain uncertain as to which specific situations represent the greatest liabilities for schizophrenia. Biologists generally take a different approach, focusing on events very early in life. Even prenatal life is seen as a source of possible stress. According to one review, inadequate maternal nutrition, maternal infection, small head size, and minor physical anomalies are all implicated in schizophrenia.[29] Other prenatal stressors linked to schizophrenia include bereavement, famine, flood, earthquake, and exposure to military conflict.[30] The evidence is especially strong for an association between schizophrenia and difficulties arising during the mother's labor or during the delivery, perhaps because problems at this critical time can reduce the amount of oxygen available to the fetus. Whatever the specific reason, the risk of schizophrenia in offspring delivered in association with obstetric problems is twice that of offspring delivered uneventfully. Interestingly, bipolar disorder and major depression are also associated with prenatal and early postnatal events.

Stress is broadly defined in biology to mean any challenge to the organism that generates a physiological response. Thus, stress interacts with disease susceptibility genes in numerous ways, depending on the nature of the diathesis and the nature of the response. In many instances, the response to stress requires the activation of genes by transcription factors. If a transcription factor is not working properly (the diathesis), the person under stress may not be able to respond effectively, thereby exposing the brain to damage. This might explain why genome-wide association studies have linked transcription factors to the risk of schizophrenia.

A specific example of early life stress concerns maternal infection. According to one hypothesis, the stress of the mother's illness is passed along to the fetus and disrupts normal development.[31] The first test of the hypothesis examined the offspring of women who were pregnant and exposed to the influenza epidemic of 1957 in Helsinki. Later, many more of these offspring developed schizophrenia than did those born in times when there was no widespread influenza. More recent studies report that the risk of schizophrenia increases five times with rubella infections; five times with maternal genital/ reproductive infections; either seven times or three times with influenza infections depending on whether the infection occurs early or late in pregnancy); and two times for infection with the parasite *Toxoplasma gondii*.[32] In related findings, recent genome-wide association studies have discovered that immunity genes are possible risk factors for schizophrenia.[33] It is conceivable, therefore, that a mutation in one or more immunity gene (the diathesis) could interact with maternal infection (the stressor) to affect the development of the brain in the fetus. Another influential hypothesis is based on the fact that stressful events trigger the release of the hormone, cortisol.[34] Cortisol affects the neurotransmitter dopamine, and dopamine has long been implicated in schizophrenia. According to this hypothesis, a dopamine system that is already functioning less than optimally due to a gene variant (the diathesis) may get into serious trouble when subjected to stress. Like the maternal infection hypothesis, the cortisol-dopamine

121

hypothesis is most plausible as a scenario unfolding during the early stages of brain development.

Recent discoveries concerning the chemistry of DNA have inspired a controversial new hypothesis to explain the interaction of genes and the environment. It turns out that genes are modified not only through mutations that change the coding sequence, but also through the attachment of chemicals, specifically methyl radicals, to the DNA comprising the gene. The phenomenon is known as *epigenetic regulation*, meaning changes in gene function that occur without changes in the underlying DNA sequence. When the radicals bind to the DNA, they make the affected genes either more or less easily activated, in some cases rendering the gene completely incapable of producing protein. The process has interesting features that could explain, or help to explain, several common diseases including schizophrenia.[35] First, because epigenetic regulation is known to occur in the human fetus, as well as at later stages, it has the potential to significantly influence brain development. Second, epigenetic regulation is sensitive to environmental events, including those that occur prenatally. Third, and perhaps most interesting, the molecular changes brought about by epigenetic mechanisms can be passed on to future generations. In this respect, epigenetic changes act like mutations, but there is a fundamental difference. Whereas mutations are transmitted reliably to offspring, the transmission of epigenetic changes is chancy. Earlier, I mentioned that the concordance rate for schizophrenia in identical twins is about 50 percent, not 100 percent as one would expect if genetics were entirely to blame. I explained that this could be due to different levels of stress experienced by the two twins. Alternatively, given the chancy nature of epigenetic inheritance, the epigenetic influence that produces schizophrenia might be unequally inherited in the two twins.

Summary and Forward Glance

The battle against mental illness stigma comprises two facets, one being the replacement of dualistic philosophies with physicalism, and the second being research to strengthen the case for a science-based psychiatry. Therefore, aside from their anticipated impacts on diagnosis and treatment, the scientific findings summarized in this chapter will influence how people think about mental illness. The point is noted by Thomas Insel, director of the National Institute of Mental Health (USA),

Perhaps the most immediate result of approaching mental disorders as brain circuit disorders will be changing public perception of these illnesses. In different generations, people with mental illness have been stigmatized as possessed, dangerous, weak-willed or victimized by bad parents. Science supports none of this. A scientific approach to mental disorders could allow those who struggle with these illnesses to receive full acceptance and the high-quality care that they deserve.[36]

The key to understanding, treating, and possibly preventing mental illness is to discover its cause or causes. Therefore, the challenge for biological psychiatry is to find the links between altered genes, biomarkers in the brain, and abnormal behaviors. The task is difficult because even the links between normal genes, normal brain organization, and normal behaviors are not fully understood. And yet, progress is definitely being made.

In my opinion, the key to future progress in schizophrenia lies in the microcircuits of the cerebral cortex, for it is there that complex synaptic interactions generate everything from conscious thoughts to limb movements. Even a slight alteration in these microcircuits—whether anatomical, chemical, or electrical—has the potential to produce psychotic behavior. I am not alone in this opinion. Two of the leading researchers in the field of biological psychiatry, Drs. P.J. Harrison of Oxford University and D.R. Weinberger of the National Institute of Mental Health (USA), emphasize the involvement of malfunctioning microcircuits in schizophrenia,

> The evidence that schizophrenia susceptibility genes affect diverse synaptic processes suggests that it will not be synapses per se but the neural circuits in which they participate which will prove to be the appropriate explanatory level to understand how the genetic influences operate. This is consistent with the view that the disorder is fundamentally one of abnormal information processing at the highest level, and such abnormalities are probably best understood in terms of malfunction of cortical micro circuits. In other words, the real locus of genetic convergence, if there is one, is downstream of any specific molecule or synaptic event per se, and resides in some integrative activity or emergent property of the circuits subserving the core cognitive elements affected in schizophrenia, for example, by impairing the signal-to-noise ratio and decreasing the efficiency of information processing.[37]

Much of what has been said here about schizophrenia also holds true for other mental illnesses. Heredity, for example, is definitely a factor

123

determining the risk for autism, bipolar disease, and major depression. Although current evidence favors the hypothesis that combinations of common gene variants are responsible for all the major mental illnesses, the alternatives of rare but potent mutations or copy number variations have not been ruled out for any illness. The susceptibility genes that have been identified for schizophrenia are predominately those that have roles in the early development and later maintenance of neural microcircuits. The same types of genes are implicated in vulnerability for autism, bipolar disease, and depression. Of special interest is the finding that some specific gene variants are associated with two or more different psychiatric illnesses.[38] One example is the gene DISC1, which I mentioned above in relation to schizophrenia; variants of this gene are also implicated in schizo-affective disorder, bipolar disorder, major depression, and autism. The genes for the zinc finger protein 804A and several cell adhesion molecules are associated with both schizophrenia and bipolar disease. These findings suggest that the major psychiatric diseases are genetically related.

The physical evidence relating to mental illness now includes DNA, neurotransmitters, and microneuroanatomy. These discoveries, together with others to follow, will inevitably lead to changes in how we diagnose mental disorders. Already, autism spectrum disorder is detected by magnetic resonance imaging in 90 percent of cases.[39] Eventually, it should be possible to discard all or most of the subjective criteria for mental diseases, now the mainstay of DSM-IV, and replace them with genetic, chemical, and anatomical criteria. The number of diagnostic errors will surely decrease as more and more of these objective criteria become available. Clinical practices will benefit, and so too will research efforts because there will be less noise in the data. Another effect of switching from subjective criteria to objective criteria will be the revision of diagnostic categories. The greater resolving power of physical evidence will undoubtedly reveal that diseases such as schizophrenia, which are now considered single diseases with widely ranging symptoms, are actually families of related diseases associated with different constellations of gene variants. A similar transformation in the diagnosis of cancer is already under way. Even the name, schizophrenia, could eventually disappear as physical descriptions take over from behavioral and psychological descriptions and the reality of new disease categories becomes apparent.

Some readers may be disquieted by a view of mental illness in which mind itself has no place. On the horizon, too, lies the prospect that mind might be banished entirely from our everyday conversations. If that were to happen, would we speak only in machine languages, or join the ranks of David Chalmers's spiritless zombies? In the previous chapter, I presented some philosophical alternatives to Cartesian dualism that would forestall such a future, but those ideas may be too arcane for everyday use. Fortunately, there are other ideas that should make it possible for us to live comfortably in a world in which there are no minds and no mental causes. As I will explain in the final chapter, it is okay to talk *as if* minds exist and mental events cause behaviors, so long as we understand that such things are not actually true.

Notes

1. Descartes, 1637. See Descartes, 1965, p. 112.
2. Malebranche, 1674, p. 88.
3. Zimmer, 2004, p. 174.
4. Ibid., p. 228.
5. Szasz, 1976, p. 105.
6. More complete accounts can be found in Harrison and Weinberger, 2005; Lisman et al., 2008; Paus et al., 2008; Insel, 2010b.
7. Harrison, 1999; Frankle et al., 2003; Arion et al., 2007.
8. More exactly, the studies measure levels of RNA specific to individual genes. Because RNA is the template from which proteins are made, the RNA provides a good estimate of protein levels.
9. American Psychiatric Association, 2000.
10. Paus et al., 2008.
11. The figures are for normal brains; data from Selemon et al., 1998.
12. Sigurdsson et al., 2010.
13. Logothetis, 2008.
14. Potkin and Ford, 2009, and accompanying articles.
15. Klempan et al., 2004.
16. Based on Klempan et al., 2004; Sanes et al., 2006.
17. Frotscher, 2010.
18. Sullivan et al., 2007.
19. Kandel, 2001.
20. Harrison and Weinberger, 2005; The International Schizophrenia Consortium, 2009; Shi et al., 2009; Stefansson et al., 2009; Insel, 2010b.
21. The International Schizophrenia Consortium, 2009.
22. Although I have written that 180 genes were identified, in fact, 180 single nucleotide polymorphisms were identified (SNPs). SNPs are variants of the single DNA letters that comprise the genetic code. Some of the SNPs were in the regulatory regions of the DNA (introns) rather than in the protein-coding regions (exons).
23. Allen et al., 2010.
24. Walsh et al., 2008.
25. Stefansson et al., 2008. However, a recent study suggests that copy number variants are "unlikely to contribute greatly to the genetic basis of common human diseases" (The Wellcome Trust Case Control Consortium, 2010).

26. Gottesman, 1991. Note that the 50 percent correlation rate for identical twins is not to be confused with the 80 percent heritability estimate; the latter is calculated from the difference between correlations for identical twins and correlations for fraternal twins.
27. Ibid.
28. Ibid., p. 91.
29. Lewis and Levitt, 2005.
30. Malaspina et al., 2008.
31. Clarke et al., 2009.
32. Brown and Derkits, 2010.
33. Stefansson et al., 2009; Shi et al., 2009.
34. Walker and Diforio, 1997.
35. Petronis, 2010; for a summary of the controversy concerning the role of epigenetics in psychiatry, see Buchen, 2010.
36. Insel, 2010a.
37. Harrison and Weinberger, 2005, pp. 56–7.
38. Hyman, 2008.
39. Ecker et al., 2010.

7

Toward a Reconciliation of Philosophy and Science in Psychiatry

The difficult problems of mind–body philosophy cause many of us, eminent thinkers included, to straddle theoretical fences. Both Réne Descartes and Sigmund Freud, two champions of the mentalist or psychological point of view, expressed decidedly physicalist thoughts at certain points in their careers. Descartes, known today for his metaphysical philosophy, had a deep interest in science and mechanics. He was inspired by the 620 water jets and the hydraulically-controlled moving statues in the French Royal Gardens to think of physiology in terms of hydraulics, and he imagined that human actions are controlled by fluids flowing through the nerves. As for his metaphysical work, it "was intended . . . to be preliminary to a larger enterprise of science, medicine, and technology, which would confer practical benefits on mankind."[1] Freud, trained in neurology and neuroanatomy, felt that psychoanalysis was but a stepping stone on the road to a biological explanation of human behavior. In one book he wrote, "The deficiencies in our description would probably vanish if we were already in a position to replace the psychological terms with physiological or chemical ones."[2] Like the rest of us, Descartes and Freud struggled to resolve "the tension between the objective world of physical existence and the subjective world of experience."[3]

The truth of the matter is that the physical and subjective worlds are not yet united in any fully satisfying philosophy. Although Cartesian dualism remains popular in the general population, most professional philosophers have abandoned it. The professional thinkers currently favor physicalism and functionalism, but heated arguments continue surrounding many key issues. Perhaps the most fundamental problem is how to square the familiar experience of consciousness with the idea that everything in the world is physical. Nowhere in society is this problem more acute than in the psychiatric community. My purpose in this chapter is to suggest ways in which psychiatry, and the broader society, can accommodate both the dualism of their intuitions and the monism of science. As part of this effort, I will be so bold as to suggest that we can accept physicalism as a philosophy of mind even while we continue to use the language of dualism in our everyday lives.

Philosophical Rumblings in the Psychiatric Community

Although the mind must be constantly on the minds of psychiatrists, few write and publish about it. However, those that do voice their opinions strike chords of discontent that resonate in the professional journals. These authors understand the need to update the philosophical underpinnings of psychiatry. One piece begins with a quotation from the well-known psychiatrist and existential philosopher, Karl Jaspers, who wrote, "Many a psychiatrist has said that he did not want to burden himself with a philosophy . . . but the exclusion of philosophy would . . . be disastrous for psychiatry."[4]

Earlier, I mentioned the lament of Sam Huber, the forth-year medical student who editorialized on how Cartesian dualism was giving psychiatry a bad reputation and turning students away from the specialty. He recommended that his professional colleagues abandon dualism in favor of a modern, physicalist philosophy. Addressing the same problem, namely the lowly status of contemporary psychiatry, Dr. Eric Kandel, a psychiatrist and celebrated neuroscientist, delivered a similar message in his important article, "A New Intellectual Framework for Psychiatry," which I mentioned briefly in chapter 2.[5] We need to consider several controversial points made by Kandel in this article.

Kandel begins by emphatically rejecting Cartesian dualism in favor of physicalism. Then, in the bulk of the article, he discusses the essential involvement of memories in mental disorders. He describes how experience affects the expression of genes, and how the protein products of these genes change microcircuits in the brain, thus producing changes in behavior. Kandel himself conducted much of the research in this area, work that earned him the Nobel Prize in Physiology or Medicine (2000).[6] Among the conclusions in this paper is that when psychiatric disorders originate from maladaptive learning, therapeutic interventions can effect clinical improvements by removing the physical traces of the "bad" memories.

Kandel's article[5] was controversial not only for its unabashed physicalism and its reductionism, but equally for its surprising closing section entitled, "Biology and the Possibility of a Renaissance of Psychoanalytic Thought." The final sentence of the article expresses the author's confidence that a biologically based psychoanalysis would "live up to its initial promise and help revolutionize our understanding of mind and brain." Responding to the large volume of correspondence generated by these comments, Kandel published a second article in the same journal to elaborate on the subject.[7] Here, his point of view is particularly revealing.

> An issue that is often raised is that a neurobiological approach to psychoanalytic issues would reduce psychoanalytic concepts to neurobiological ones. If that were so, it would deprive psychoanalysis of its essential texture and richness and change the character of therapy. Such a reduction is not simply undesirable but impossible. The agendas for psychoanalysis, cognitive psychology, and neural science overlap, but they are by no means identical.[8]

So, Kandel, the scientist who gained fame by researching synapses and genes, proclaims psychoanalysis as an *irreducible* platform from which to investigate mind and brain. What is going on here? Obviously, he does not think that physicalism is enough. He wants physicalism for some purposes, psychoanalysis for others. To appreciate his stance, we need to recall the different meanings of *reduction*, discussed in chapter 5. According to the definitions given there, Kandel is a metaphysical reductionist and a methodological reductionist, but not an explanatory reductionist. That is, while he rejects mind as a metaphysical entity, he uses nonphysical concepts and nonphysical language to explain human behavior. More accurately, Kandel prefers to use *both* biological explanations *and* psychological explanations. As I will show below, he is not alone among mental health professionals in seeking to explain mental illness from multiple perspectives. A realistic understanding of mental illness requires both reductionist explanations *and* nonreductionist explanations.

Another psychiatrist promoting a combination of reductionist and nonreductionist explanations is Dr. Kenneth S. Kendler, the distinguished professor of psychiatry at the Medical College of Virginia and a leading researcher in psychiatric genetics. Kendler calls upon his colleagues to replace Cartesian dualism with what he calls *explanatory pluralism*, an approach emphasizing "multiple mutually informative perspectives."[9] It is especially appropriate for psychiatry, he writes, because mental illnesses are caused by "processes operating at several levels of abstraction." Even while acknowledging the roles played by genes and neurochemical alterations, Kendler argues that psychological, cultural, and social factors should also be considered.

Taking a somewhat different approach, yet one that also incorporates both reductionist and nonreductionist explanations, two authors writing in the *British Medical Journal* stress the relevance of *meanings* in relation to the mind–body problem. Patrick Bracken and Philip Thomas insist that "[c]onceptualizing our mental life as some sort of enclosed world residing inside the skull does not do justice to the lived reality of human experience. It systematically neglects the importance of social context."[10] To illustrate their point, they ask us to recall the painting *Guernica* by Pablo Picasso, which depicts human suffering during the Spanish Civil War.

> How do we understand and appreciate this? The type of pigment is important, as are the brushstrokes used. So too are the colors and the shapes of the figures. But to understand what the painting means and the genius of its creator we reach beyond the canvas itself to the context in which it was created. This entails historical, political, cultural, and personal dimensions. Without engaging with its context, we could never appreciate "Guernica" as a work of genius. Its meaning does not reside in the pigment or the canvas but in the relation between these and the world in which it was created and now exists.[11]

Thus, drawing upon the lessons of art, and citing the philosophers Wittgenstein and Heidegger, Bracken and Thomas declare that psychiatry should embrace a meanings-based perspective on mental illness so as to better "comprehend [the] fundamental aspects of human suffering." They close by remarking, "Signs are encouraging that psychiatrists are becoming interested in philosophy. But the rest of medicine also needs to get beyond the legacy of Descartes."

Similar ideas are developed in greater detail by the philosophically inclined psychologists Derek Bolton and Jonathan Hill. In their book, *Mind, Meaning, and Mental Disorder*,[12] these men emphasize the importance of meaning, not just as a mental concept but also as a biological concept. They claim that all biological systems must incorporate meanings, for otherwise they would not function correctly. Taking as their example the system regulating blood pressure, they argue that the body must "know" that a high frequency of action potentials in certain nerves *means* high blood pressure and that high blood pressure *means* that a corrective nerve message must be sent to command the dilation of blood vesicles. Because meanings are encoded in the brain, they say, meanings can cause physical actions. They describe some rules that biological systems use when processing meaningful information, and they write about the medical consequences when the rules are corrupted or impaired. Such rules, they say, can be adversely affected either through physical interruptions, for example from strokes, or by nonphysical means such as "persistent misinterpretations of the actions of others, recurrent thoughts that [do] not match external circumstances, and persistent mood change that is disproportionate to a person's condition."[13] In other words, when corrupted rules lead to consistent misinterpretations, the result can be mental illness.

All of the views summarized above seek an escape from the dichotomous thinking that stems from the separation of mind and brain. Earlier, I identified two medical dichotomies, namely the distinction between *mental and physical* diseases (already implicit in Plato's writings) and the distinction between *voluntary and involuntary* diseases (common in the nineteenth century). A third dichotomy, not previously mentioned, is the distinction between *functional and organic* psychiatric illnesses. According to this idea, first introduced in the mid-nineteenth century, an illness is said to be organic if it is consistently associated with a demonstrable brain abnormality (e.g., Alzheimer's disease and degeneration due to toxic reactions), whereas in the absence of such evidence (e.g., schizophrenia and depression), it is labeled as functional. In effect, the terms *mental, voluntary,* and *functional* all carry the same meaning, namely, an illness of the mind, whereas the terms *physical, involuntary,* and *organic* signify an illness of the body.

Psychiatrists today tend to be uncomfortable with all the preceding dichotomies. Instead of forced-choice alternatives, they look for pluralistic perspectives. They acknowledge the biological underpinnings of mental illness, but they want *additional* interpretations, ones that speak to them in languages other than that of science. I have described some representative outlooks in the paragraphs above. To emphasize the common elements in these propositions, I have crudely summarized the views of the key authors in Table 7.1.

Table 7.1   A summary of contemporary proposals that avoid both dualism
and strict physicalism

Kandel (1998)	Psychiatry can accommodate both psychoanalysis and neural science
Bracken and Thomas (2002)	Psychiatry needs a meanings-based perspective
Bolton and Hill (2003)	Mental illness results from the corruption of rules for processing meanings
Kendler (2005)	Psychiatry needs multiple, mutually informative perspectives

Interestingly, the current discussion among psychiatrists parallels a similar debate within academic philosophy. In the latter case, the specific issue is how to reconcile the sophisticated, physicalist theories of mind with the use of nonphysicalist concepts in areas of scholarship such as psychology, economics, and anthropology, fields collectively known as the social sciences. It is common for these disciplines to use language that references mental states and abstract ideas, which is to say these disciplines use concepts that cannot be reduced to the terms of physics. Because physics requires reduction, whereas the social sciences do not, philosophers call the latter disciplines *special sciences*. Psychiatry is neither an ordinary science nor a special science, strictly speaking, but it too is looking for a way to incorporate seemingly irreducible concepts into a physicalist framework. Therefore, it will be useful to consider how philosophers justify the use of irreducible concepts in the special sciences. It may be that the allowances made by philosophers for the special sciences can serve equally well to legitimize the use of nonphysical explanations in psychiatry.

Mental Causation is Okay in the "Special Sciences"

In chapter 5, I concluded that mental events (and mental states) probably do not cause anything to happen, not even other mental events. Only physical events, including the neuronal representations of mental events, can cause things to happen. I reached these conclusions because to do otherwise would return us to a form of dualism. Nevertheless, I must admit that this morning, when playing tennis, I told my partner that I was hitting the ball well because I was playing *with confidence*. Confidence is a mental state, so how can it affect what happens to the tennis ball? Not only that, but I told my friend that I *tried* to hit the ball in the corner and that I *intentionally* hit it hard. Like you the reader, like all of us, I speak the language of folk psychology.

Psychiatrists, too, customarily use language that implies mental causation. They discuss their patient's state of mind, and they say things like, "She became *depressed* when she *realized* that he *did not love her.*" And, "The killer was driven by his *fear* of failure." Can we reconcile the utterance of such statements with our understanding, from logical arguments, that mental events and mental states are incapable of causing anything to happen? Several contemporary philosophers say that it is okay to use psychological language, even folk psychology, to explain human behaviors. We can do this, they say, even while we insist that all events must have physical causes.

One approach to justifying the use of psychological or mental language is to employ the so-called *dual explanandum strategy.*[14] Consider these two explanations for why a man suddenly launched a violent attack against a competitor. We could say that, in the brain of the attacker, there was an excess of potassium ions in a certain microcircuit that caused a few key neurons to fire action potentials when normally they would have remained silent. Equally, we could attribute the attack to the man's belief that his thoughts were being read by an electronic receiver embedded in the teeth of the competitor.[15] In this example, the first explanation is strictly physicalist, whereas the second is couched in psychological terms.

The philosophical justification for the dual explanandum strategy rests on certain fundamental differences between physics and the other sciences, particularly psychology. One difference is that the facts and laws of physics are completely covered by physics itself, whereas psychology often draws upon knowledge in related fields such as (neuro)physiology, (neuro)chemistry, and genetics. Moreover, the explanations of psychological states often take into account external factors such as the person's situation relative to the economy, the weather, political happenings, and so on. In sum, physics is *self-contained*, whereas psychology is not.

Another big difference between physics and psychology concerns what can and what cannot be reduced. Physics, of course, is the base to which all phenomena are supposed to reduce. Neurons fire action potentials when the membrane potential depolarizes sufficiently to trigger the opening of voltage-gated ion channels in the cell membrane, thereby allowing sodium ions to flow down their concentration gradient into the cell. In this example, as in all of physics, a single explanation suffices. By contrast, according to the arguments of Jerry Fodor,[16] psychological explanations are never singular, that is, there are always multiple ways in which a given psychological phenomenon can be reduced to other, lower level phenomena. The situation, you may recognize, is one of *multiple realization*.[17] In the example given earlier, no single physical account of pain will suffice for all instances of pain (human pain as well as octopus pain) because different nervous elements are likely to be responsible (C-fibers in humans, X-fibers in octopuses). Similarly, it does not seem possible to explain paranoia by reference to any *particular* set of synapses or any *particular* group of neurons because each instance of paranoia will be different in its history, contents, and context. By the same logic, depression, anxiety, and all other mental states are multiply realized in different individuals.

Jerry Fodor and others conclude that no science besides physics is self-contained and fully reducible. Therefore, they say, psychology, together with most other sciences whether "social" or not, must be designated *a special science,* whereas physics is just . . . physics.[18] Because the concepts of the special sciences are multiply realizable, hence not fully reducible, the special sciences are licensed to use types of explanation that are prohibited in physics. This is good, for otherwise it would be difficult to talk about mental illness, let alone describe one's tennis match.

Some readers may protest that the dual explanandum strategy is little more than an abstract philosophical argument invented to resolve an artificial problem. To say this, however, is to deny the real contradiction between the common attributions of mental causation evident in our everyday conversations and the attractive theory of mind known as physicalism. It is the job of philosophy to sort out conundrums of this kind; I will therefore summarize two additional arguments that philosophers use to support the dual explanandum strategy. First, because causation is not the same as explanation, we can *explain* a behavior by referring to conflicts, beliefs, feelings, or pains without granting these mental states *causal* powers.[19] For example, we send rocket ships into deep space because we are ambitious, we need adventure, and there is the potential for economic benefit. Although all of these reasons count as explanations, none qualifies as a cause of the rocket ship lifting off from its launch pad; for that one needs to ignite the fuel and start the engines. Similarly, an unconscious conflict[20] may explain Fred's angry outburst, but it is the nerve impulses in Fred's vagus nerve that cause sounds to issue from his mouth.

Another way to reconcile the use of mental language while insisting on the primacy of physical causation is to appeal to what one philosopher calls *transparency*. Frank Jackson notes that we typically explain human behaviors by telling stories, and he stresses that two types of stories are available for use.[21] Stories based on physical causation are "the real McCoy," whereas stories based on mental causation are only approximations of the truth. Both types of explanations are acceptable because, while the causes are always physical, the mechanisms in a particular case may be difficult to describe or the details may be unknown. Jackson finds no problem with using psychological terms as a kind of shorthand reference to the physical causes, so long as we are honest (transparent) about how the two types of stories relate to each other.

> [T]he story transparency theorists tell about mental causation has essentially a dual character: there is a part that tells how behaviour, internal states and surroundings, all described in physical language—as neurostates playing certain functional roles, as sentences of mentalese, as stimulations of sense organs by the environment, as movements of limbs, and the like—causally interconnect, and there is a part that tells about which of these goings on should be described in psychological terms—which neurostates or functional states are to be called beliefs, which limb movements are to be called actions, and so on. Why does this mean that the physical story counts as the real McCoy? Because (of course) calling something a belief or an action does not affect its causal powers or ancestry.[22]

To summarize, modern philosophy may take away our belief in mental causation, but it does not deny us the use of mental explanations in the special sciences. Metaphysical reduction continues to be practiced, while explanatory reduction and methodological reduction remain options. The message for psychiatry, I believe, is that psychological explanations have their place, but one should not forget that the actual causes of mental illness are biological. Effective treatments depend on changing the physical brain, so therapies need to be directed to those aspects of the nervous system that are disrupted by the illness. Eric Kandel explains how the "new intellectual framework" for psychiatry contrasts with earlier views:

> The distinction [functional disorders and organic disorders], now clearly outdated, is no longer tenable. There can be no changes in behavior that are not reflected in the nervous system and no persistent changes in the nervous system that are not reflected in structural changes on some level of resolution. . . .We no longer think that only certain diseases, the organic diseases, affect mentation through biological changes in the brain and that others, the functional diseases, do not. The basis of the new intellectual framework for psychiatry is that all mental processes are biological, and therefore any alteration in those processes is necessarily organic.[23]

Kandel does not hesitate to assert that all physical interventions, including pharmacological treatments, produce changes in the brain, often at synapses. Moreover, he says, "Insofar as psychotherapy is successful in bringing about substantive changes in behavior, it does so by producing alterations in gene expression that produce new structural changes in the brain."[24] In his view, psychotherapy is a learning experience and, like all learning experiences, it creates memories at synapses.[25] When psychological talk works, it does so by changing synapses. In short, whether it is talk therapy, medication, electrical stimulation, or something else, to change behavior one must change the brain.

Do We Need to Rename Mental Illness?

I have argued that the term mental illness is a misnomer. Does it therefore make sense to replace mental illness with another term? The answer, I suggest, is yes, but it is not likely to happen soon. If I had been in a rush to eliminate the term, I would have done so at the beginning of this book, but the fact of the matter is that it would have been difficult. Emily Brontë's expression has not only been accepted, it has become firmly embedded in our discourse. However, a recently introduced modification has garnered attention.

Beginning in the 1960s, persons working in the mental health profession began using the term *mental disorder* as a substitute for *mental illness*. Coincidentally—or not—the word change occurred at the height of the so-called antipsychiatry movement, following the publication of Thomas Szasz's book, *The Myth of Mental Illness*, in 1961.[26] In any event, the medical profession, if not the general public, now seems to prefer disorder over illness. Consider, as evidence, the title of the standard reference text, the *Diagnostic and Statistical Manual of Mental Disorders* (DSM-IV). Most of the syndromes described therein are named disorders, for example bipolar disorder, schizotypal personality disorder, obsessive-compulsive personality disorder, etc. The Introduction to the DSM-IV contains an apology of sorts, declaring that "[t]he problem raised by the term 'mental disorder' has been much clearer than its solution, and, unfortunately, the term persists in the title of DSM-IV because we have not found an appropriate substitute."[27] Likewise, the World Health Organization's *International Classification of Diseases* (ICD, tenth edition) uses the term by default and with a similar apology. Their Introduction states, "The term 'disorder' is used throughout the classification, so as to avoid even greater problems inherent in the use of terms such as 'disease' and 'illness'. 'Disorder' is not an exact term."[28]

What, then, to call the conditions currently known as mental illness/mental disorder? This question has become controversial within the psychiatric community. One commentator has gone so far as to describe the situation as a "terminological power struggle."[29] Obviously, the issue concerns the very nature of the conditions, and it involves such fundamental questions as to whether the conditions are actual illnesses. Some critics, like the psychiatrist and philosopher, Derek Bolton, reject the medical model on the grounds that it too strongly endorses the physicalist point of view. According to Bolton, the medical model implicitly ignores psychological and psychosocial explanations.[30] Other critics accept the medical model but contend that it is impossible to distinguish the so-called mental illnesses from the so-called physical illnesses.[31] "In reality," says Dr. R.E. Kendell, "neither minds nor bodies develop illnesses. Only people . . . do so, and when they do both mind and body, psyche and soma are usually involved."[32] In a similar vein, the DSM-IV comments, "The term mental disorder unfortunately implies a distinction between 'mental' disorders and 'physical' disorders that is a reductionistic anachronism of mind/body dualism."[33] Notwithstanding the questionable reference to a "reductionistic anachronism," the DSM-IV seems to agree with Kendell's view that mind and body are inseparable in disease. But, while Kendell recommends the term *psychiatric illness*, the DSM-IV sticks with *mental disorder*.

For physicalists who believe that the so-called mental diseases are actually brain diseases, the continued use of the former term is reprehensible and scientifically invalid. It is reprehensible because it contributes to stigmatization, and it is invalid because it does not identify the true nature of the conditions. Here is how Baker and

Menken, writing in the British Medical Journal, make their case for eliminating the label mental illness:

> Our reflection upon the stigma and prejudice that apply differentially to people with nervous systems disorders have led us to conclude that the mental health and mental illness labels traditionally and commonly used to characterize certain brain disorders contribute to these twin sources of unnecessary suffering . . . . Advances in neuroscience during the past 50 years have left us not knowing how or where to draw a line between brain and mental problems, or between psychiatric and neurological disorders, as is customarily done. From our angle of vision, there are only brain disorders that psychiatrists prefer to treat and other brain disorders that neurologists (and neurosurgeons) prefer to treat.[34]

Thus, motivated by the need to reduce stigma and prejudice, Baker and Menken advocate replacing mental illness with *brain disorder*. The National Alliance on Mental Illness has likewise campaigned to change the emphasis from mind to brain, and for the same reason, but their efforts are stymied by the fact that the very name of their organization includes the words "mental illness"!

My own objection to the term mental illness is that it implies the existence of a mind that becomes ill. If there are anachronisms of medical terminology, this is surely one of them. To continue using the term is to deny advances in both science and philosophy. I have little doubt that a term like brain illness will ultimately prevail, but it may be unwise to force the issue at this time. Although academics and professionals are beginning to prefer the term brain illness (or its equivalent) instead of its predecessor, mental illness, usage in the general population lags behind. A major reason for this difference is that the public still struggles to appreciate the biological nature of the major psychiatric syndromes.

Certain linguistic strategies can be employed while transiting to a world in which mental illness, so-described, no longer exists. One idea is to forego all manner of classification, as recommended by Derek Bolton.[35] He would have us refer to each condition by its individual name, for example, schizophrenia, depression, autism, etc. Some individual conditions could continue to carry the label disorder, as in bipolar disorder, but the category term, mental disorder, would be discarded. Alternatively, following Kendell[36] and Baker and Menken,[37] we could name medical conditions according to the professional disciplines that customarily treat them. Thus, instead of mental diseases and brain diseases, we would have psychiatric diseases and neurological diseases. This is a pragmatic solution that side-steps the philosophical issues, but it perpetuates an arbitrary distinction between types of brain diseases.

Perhaps the best near-term solution is to adopt the name *neuropsychiatric disease,* a label that is already in use at some institutions. It is somewhat vague, and it can be criticized for retaining a reference to mind in the guise of its Latin equivalent, but it narrows the gap between mental conditions and nervous conditions. Moreover, it beckons psychiatry and neuroscience to join forces in developing strategies for prevention and treatment.

Consequences for Attitudes and Worldviews

Society will experience significant changes as the belief in Cartesian dualism declines in the face of scientific advances. One important change will occur in attitudes towards persons with mental illness. Current public opinion polls show that a significant percentage of the population thinks that individuals with mental illnesses are personally responsible for their conditions. I reviewed these data in chapter 2. One survey found that 38 percent of respondents think that major depression "might be caused by" the person's "own bad character"; another survey found that 50 percent of respondents believe that schizophrenia is caused by a "lack of will power"; a third survey reported that 46 percent of respondents agree that mental illness is "an excuse for poor behavior." Fortunately, we can expect to see a gradual reduction in these points of view as the physicalist philosophy gains ground on dualism. It will be difficult to hold people responsible for their illnesses if it is known that they were caused by defective mechanisms of brain development.

The public opinion surveys mentioned above asked mainly about major depression and schizophrenia. They do not reveal attitudes toward agoraphobia, depersonalization disorder, hypochondriasis, voyeurism, or any of the other conditions listed among the 297 "disorders" in the DSM-IV. Science has so far associated only a very few of these conditions with faulty genes, abnormal brain development, or altered microcircuits. Many people no doubt see these disorders as mere *neuroses* (now an obsolete term in psychiatry) and, following Sigmund Freud, they interpret them psychologically. This way of thinking facilitates attributions of personal responsibility and contributes to stigmatization. By contrast, the physicalist point of view maintains that *all* mental disorders are caused by the combined influences of genes and the environment, even if the specific causes have not yet been identified. It follows that no person with a mental illness—regardless of its nature—should be held responsible for the illness. One hopes, therefore, that the wider acceptance of physicalism will bring more tolerance and less moral judgment to those suffering from mental illness.

We can also expect that our changing attitudes toward mental illness will impact the criminal justice system. Earlier, I cited the M'Naghten rule, which allows for a verdict of "not guilty" in cases where the accused did not know "the nature and quality of the act he was doing; or if he did know it, that he did not know he was doing what was wrong." In today's courts, the so-called insanity defense is infrequently invoked and even more rarely successful. One might ask, with reason, whether the M'Naghten rule has become obsolete as a guideline for decision-making in cases involving psychiatric illness and, if it is, what rule might best replace it. The issue is one of responsibility, and the resolution depends on one's position with respect to free will. While philosophers argue vociferously about free will, most mainstream contemporary philosophers, even the physicalists, think that there is a sense in which people should be held responsible for their actions. The favored test is whether an actor "could have done otherwise." Unfortunately, for reasons both practical and logical, the test is not easily administered.[38]

I think that the advance of neuroscience, together with the concurrent decline of dualism, will progressively reduce the frequency of attributions of responsibility in criminal cases because brain mechanisms will replace free will as the assumed cause. In my opinion, it is right to acquit persons of acts that would otherwise be considered unlawful if it can be shown that the accused has a mis-wired or malfunctioning brain. It should be the duty of the court to decide, after listening to arguments from the defense and the prosecution, whether the brain in question is, in fact, mis-wired or malfunctioning. Under current practice, acquittals are rarely granted except in cases of documented delusions, hallucinations, or epileptic seizures. I expect, however, that the psychiatric defense in criminal cases will gradually expand to include many conditions not currently considered eligible. Society should be protected from dangerous individuals, but no one should be punished for acts that they cannot avoid. In a similar vein, a leading neuroscientist has recently called for abandoning the notion of free will and stopping the incarceration of persons found guilty of criminal acts. Anthony Cashmore would grant exceptions only in special cases, namely, when incarceration is necessary to protect society, to protect the offending individuals from society, to provide psychiatric help, to act as a deterrent, or to alleviate the pain of the victim.[39]

In effect, there are two opposing views about criminal justice: one says that *everyone* guilty of a crime should be punished regardless of his or her brain condition, whereas the other says that *no one* should be punished even if they have a fully normal brain. While current practice favors the former view, I believe that future policies and practices will lean more heavily towards the latter view.

Separate, but not too distant from our concerns over mental illness, lurking beneath the philosophical debates, is a battle of world views. It is a clash between spirituality and materialism, and it is heating up. In earlier times, it was customary to interpret natural phenomena in light of one's religious beliefs. Scientists constituted only a small minority of the total population, and they generally stuck to themselves. Even if a scientist had doubts about religion—and few actually did—these concerns were rarely voiced owing to a fear of social backlash. Now things are different, and scientists frequently clash with religious fundamentalists. While the debate over evolution and creationism has received the most attention, several astute observers have noted that the disagreements are broader and deeper. For example, at the annual meeting of the American Association for the Advancement of Science, held in Boston in early 2008, a panel of experts discussed how scientists could best make their case for Darwinian evolution and against Creationism. As it turned out, the least interesting aspects of the discussion concerned questions of strategy and technique. The discussion moderator, David Goldston, noted allusions to a far more significant issue, as he explained in *Nature* magazine.

> [T]he panelists tiptoed around the fact that scientific discovery can genuinely undermine religious beliefs. The focus of the panel was on teaching evolution, but discoveries in genetics and neuroscience are likely to be far more problematic in the long run. The two fields are verging on drawing the ultimate materialist picture of human nature—humans as nothing more than proteins and electrical impulses, all machine and no ghost, to play off Descartes' formulation. This view will challenge not only fundamentalist views about the soul, but more widely held notions about what it means to be

141

a person. That will further complicate age-old questions about the nature of individual responsibility and morality.[40]

Paul Bloom, the developmental psychologist and author of *Descartes' Baby*, has also commented on the power of ideas to first shake and then shape a society's outlook on life. Writing in the *New York Times*, he offered this opinion in reference to the rise of physicalist/materialist views:

> The conclusion that our souls are flesh is profoundly troubling to many, as it clashes with the notion that the soul survives the death of the body. It is a much harder pill to swallow than evolution, then, and might be impossible to reconcile with many religious views. This clash is not going to be easily resolved. The great conflict between science and religion in the last century was over evolutionary biology. In this century, it will be over psychology, and the stakes are nothing less than our souls.[41]

Bloom refers to a coming conflict between science and religion in which the stakes will be "nothing less than our souls." Nearly 400 years ago, René Descartes may well have anticipated a similar conflict as he sat down to write his famous essays. In his day, too, science had captured the popular imagination, and it was beginning to threaten the inviolability of the soul. Descartes' dualism was an inspired invention, perfectly suited to meet the needs of a troubled populace. Unlike animals, he said, humans have not just a body, but also a soul. Because the soul, or mind, is independent of the body—indeed, powerful over it—humans are free. Thus, he brilliantly conceived a philosophy that exalted mankind's unique status while confirming the church's teachings. Today, with science more sophisticated and more powerful than in Descartes' time, religion is once again threatened. Curiously, though, religion is also in high demand.

Because spirituality and physicalism stand opposed to one another, it is ironic that supernatural beliefs and practices are becoming more popular in those very societies that have the most advanced scientific cultures. The anthropologist Pascal Boyer has an explanation. He credits modern science for evoking

> a strong impulse to find at least *one* domain where it would be possible to trump the scientists. Life used to be one such domain, as scientists could not properly explain in a purely physical way

the difference between living and nonliving things or the evolution of exquisitely designed organisms. Life had to be special, perhaps the effect of some nonphysical vital élan or energy. But evolution and microbiology crushed all of this and showed that life is indeed a physical phenomenon. All that is left, for some people, is the *soul*, and the idea that mental events, thoughts and memories and emotions, are not *just* physical events in brains.[42]

Given this deep-seated belief in nonmaterial forces and entities, and recognizing the role played by religion in catering to these beliefs, it is reasonable to ask what will happen to religion as dualism fades away. In its institutionalized forms, at least, religion is already on the decline. The social scientist, Steve Bruce, has documented a history of secularization, defined by him as the "long-term decline in the power, popularity, and prestige of religious beliefs and rituals."[43] Citing census data and other research conducted in Great Britain, Bruce tells us that church attendance declined from about 50 percent of the adult population in 1851 to 7.5 percent in 1998. In the United Kingdom (Great Britain plus Northern Ireland), church memberships declined from 27 percent of the total population in 1900 to 10 percent in 2000. The Church of England baptized 63 percent of English babies in the period 1895–1950, but 53 percent in 1962, and only 27 percent in 1993. When asked, in the 1950s, whether they believed in God, only 2 percent of British adults replied that they did not, but by the 1990s, the percentage of nonbelievers had risen to 27 percent.[44]

Pascal Boyer specializes in analyzing the cognitive roots of human beliefs. Commenting on the prospect that religion might completely disappear from our cultural landscape, he notes,

> Some form of religious thinking seems to be the path of least resistance for our cognitive systems. By contrast, disbelief is generally the result of deliberate, effortful work against our natural cognitive dispositions—hardly the easiest ideology to propagate.[45]

If Boyer is right—and his intuitions appear sound—religious beliefs will persist even as science advances. Dualism, as well, is likely to have staying power because it too has roots in "natural cognitive dispositions." All of this suggests that the clash between monism and dualism, like that between science and spirituality, will likely intensify before it is resolved, and neither conflict will end any time soon

Notes

1. Williams, 1978, p. 31.
2. Freud, 1920.
3. Jaegwon Kim, from the quotation in chapter 5, p. 76.
4. Kendler, 2005. The quotation is from K. Jaspers, *General Psychopathology*, 1963, p. 769.
5. Kandel, 1998, p. 460.
6. Kandel, 2001.
7. Kandel, 1999.
8. Ibid., p. 519.
9. Kendler, 2005, p. 434.
10. Bracken and Thomas, 2002, p. 1434.
11. Ibid., p. 1433.
12. Bolton and Hill, 2003.
13. Ibid., p. xxxviii.
14. Robb and Heil, J. Mental Causation, *The Stanford Encyclopedia of Philosophy* (Summer 2009), E.N. Zalta (ed.), http://plato.stanford.edu/archives/sum2009/entries/mental-causation/.
15. Note that the latter explanation is an example of inappropriate information processing, such as described by Bolton and Hill; see my summary of their ideas above.
16. Fodor, 1974.
17. See chapter 5. p. 82.
18. Fodor, 1974.
19. The possibility of distinguishing causation and explanation is discussed in Bennett, 2007, and Robb and Heil, J. Mental Causation, *The Stanford Encyclopedia of Philosophy* (Summer 2009), E.N. Zalta (ed.), http://plato.stanford.edu/archives/sum2009/entries/mental-causation/.
20. Freud's concept; see chapter 3, p. 38.
21. Jackson, 1996.
22. Ibid., p. 379.
23. Kandel, 1998, p. 464.
24. Ibid., pp. 465–66.
25. Kandel, 2001.
26. Szasz, 1961.
27. American Psychiatric Association, 2000, p. xxx.
28. http://www.who.int/classifications/icd/en/.
29. Attributed to Graham Thornicroft in Bolton, 2008, p. 247.
30. Bolton, 2008.
31. Cooper, 2007; Baker and Menken, 2001.
32. Kendell, 2001, p. 491.
33. American Psychiatric Association, 2000, p. xxx.
34. Baker and Menken, 2001, p. 937.
35. Bolton, 2008.
36. Kendell, 2001.
37. Baker and Menken, 2001
38. For discussions of this and related issues, see Dennett, 1984; Gazzaniga, 2005.

39. Cashmore, 2010.
40. Goldston, 2008.
41. Bloom, 2004b.
42. Boyer, 2001, p. 76.
43. Bruce, 2002, p. 44.
44. Ibid., pp. 63–72.
45. Boyer, 2008, p. 1039.

Bibliography

Allen, H. L. et al. "Hundreds of Variants Clustered in Genomic Loci and Biological Pathways Affect Human Height." *Nature* 467 (2010): 832–8.

American Psychiatric Association. *Diagnostic and Statistical Manual of Mental Disorders, Fourth Edition, Text Revision.* Washington, DC: American Psychiatric Association, 2000.

Angermeyer, M. C. and H. Matschinger. "Lay Beliefs about Schizophrenic Disorder: The Results of a Population Survey in Germany." *Acta Psychiatrica Scandinavica* 89, suppl. 382 (1994): 39–45.

———. "Causal Beliefs and Attitudes to People with Schizophrenia." *British Journal of Psychiatry* 186 (2005): 331–4.

Arion, D. et al. "Molecular Evidence for Increased Expression of Genes Related to Immune and Chaperone Function in the Prefrontal Cortex in Schizophrenia." *Biological Psychiatry* 62 (2007): 711–21.

Baker, M. and M. Menken. "Time to Abandon the Term Mental Illness." *British Medical Journal* 322 (2001): 937.

Baron-Cohen, S. *Mindblindness: An Essay on Autism and Theory of Mind.* Cambridge, MA: MIT Press, 1995.

Barrett, J. L. and F. C. Keil. "Conceptualizing a Non-natural Entity: Anthropomorphism in God Concepts." *Cognitive Psychology* 31 (1996): 219–47.

Beauregard, M. and D. O'Leary. *The Spiritual Brain: A Neuroscientist's Case for the Existence of the Soul.* New York, NY: Harper Collins, 2007.

Bennett, K. "Mental Causation." *Philosophy Compass* 2 (2007): 316–37.

Bering, J. M. and D. F. Bjorkland. "The Natural Emergence of Reasoning about the Afterlife as a Developmental Regularity." *Developmental Psychology* 40 (2004): 217–33.

Bloom, P. *Descartes' Baby: How the Science of Child Development Explains What Makes Us Human.* New York, NY: Basic Books, 2004a.

———. The Dual between Body and Soul. *New York Times,* September 10, 2004b.

Bolton, D. *What Is Mental Disorder? An Essay in Philosophy, Science, and Values.* New York, NY: Oxford University Press, 2008.

Bolton, D. and J. Hill. *Mind, Meaning, and Mental Disorder: The Nature of Causal Explanation in Psychology and Psychiatry.* 2nd ed. New York, NY: Oxford University Press, 2003.

Boorse, C. "On the Distinction between Disease and Illness." *Philosophy and Public Affairs* 5 (1975): 49–68.

Boyer, P. *Religion Explained: The Evolutionary Origins of Religious Thought.* New York, NY: Basic Books, 2001.

———. "Religion: Bound to Believe?" *Nature* 455 (2008): 1038–9.

Bracken, P. and P. Thomas. "Time to Move Beyond the Mind-Body Split." *British Medical Journal* 325 (2002): 1433–4.

Brewin, C. R. "Perceived Controllability of Life-Events and Willingness to Prescribe Psychotropic Drugs." *British Journal of Social Psychology* 23 (1984): 285–7.

Broucek, F. J. *Shame and the Self.* New York, NY: Guilford Press, 1991.

Brown, A. S. and J. Derkits. "Prenatal Infection and Schizophrenia: A Review of Epidemiologic and Translational Studies." *American Journal of Psychiatry* 167 (2010): 261–80.

Bruce, S. *God is Dead: Secularization in the West.* Oxford, UK: Blackwell Publishing, 2002.

Buchen, L. "In Their Nurture." *Nature* 467 (2010): 146–8.

Cashmore, A. R. "The Lucretian Swerve: The Biological Basis of Human Behavior and the Criminal Justice System." *Proceedings of the National Academy of Sciences USA* 107 (2010): 4499–504.

Chalmers, D. J. *The Conscious Mind: In Search of a Fundamental Theory.* New York, NY: Oxford University Press, 1996.

———. "'Consciousness and the Philosophers': An Exchange." *New York Review of Books* 44, no. 8 (1997): 60–1.

Churchland, P. *Neurophilosophy: Toward a Unified Science of the Mind/Brain.* Cambridge, MA: MIT Press, 1986.

Clarke, M. C. et al. "Evidence for an Interaction between Familial Liability and Prenatal Exposure to Infection in the Causation of Schizophrenia." *American Journal of Psychiatry* 166 (2009): 1025–30.

Cooper, R. *Psychiatry and Philosophy of Science.* Montreal and Kingston: McGill–Queen's University Press, 2007.

Corrigan, P. W. et al. "Mental Illness Stigma: Problem of Public Health or Social Justice?" *Social Work* 50 (2005): 363–8.

Crandall, C. S. and D. Moriarty. "Physical Illness Stigma and Social Rejection." *British Journal of Social Psychology* 34 (1995): 67–83.

Crick, F. *The Astonishing Hypothesis: The Scientific Search for the Soul.* New York, NY: Scribner, 1994.

Damasio, A. R. *Descartes' Error: Emotion, Reason and the Human Brain.* New York, NY: Putnam, 2005.

Davidson, D. "Mental Events." In *Essays on Actions and Events*, 207–27. Oxford: Oxford University Press, 1980. First published in 1970.

Dennett, D. C. *Elbow Room: The Varieties of Free Will Worth Wanting.* Cambridge, MA: MIT Press, 1984.

———. *Consciousness Explained.* New York, NY: Back Bay Books, 1991.

———. *Breaking the Spell: Religion as a Natural Phenomenon.* New York, NY: Penguin Books, 2007.

Descartes, R. *A Discourse on Method and Other Works.* Edited by J. Epstein. New York, NY: Washington Square Press, 1965.

Ecker, C. et al. "Describing the Brain in Autism in Five Dimensions— Magnetic Resonance Imaging-Assisted Diagnosis of Autism Spectrum Disorder Using a Multiparameter Classification Approach." *Journal of Neuroscience* 30 (2010): 10612–23.

Elbogen, E. B. and S. C. Johnson. "The Intricate Link between Violence and Mental Disorder." *Archives of General Psychiatry* 66 (2009): 152–61.

Embree, R. A. and M. C. Embree. "The Personal Beliefs Scale as a Measure of Individual Differences in Commitment to the Mind-body Beliefs Proposed by F. F. Centore." *Psychological Reports* 73 (1993): 413–28.

Enard, E. et al. "Molecular Evolution of *FOXP2:* A Gene Involved in Speech and Language." *Nature* 418 (2002): 869–72.

Estes, D., H. M. Wellman and J. D. Woolley. Children's Understanding of Mental Phenomena." *Advances in Child Development and Behavior* 22 (1998): 41–87.

Fabrega Jr., H. "The Self and Schizophrenia: A Cultural Perspective." *Schizophrenia Bulletin* 15 (1989): 277–90.

Flew, A. *An Introduction to Western Philosophy: Ideas and Argument from Plato to Sartre.* London: Thames and Hudson, 1971.

Fodor, J. A. "Special Sciences (Or: The Disunity of Science as a Working Hypothesis)." *Synthese* 28 (1974): 97–115.

———. "The Mind-body Problem." *Scientific American* 244 (1981): 114–23.

Foster, J. *The Immaterial Self: A Defence of the Cartesian Dualist Conception of the Mind.* Oxford: Oxford University Press, 1991.

Foucault, M. *Madness and Civilization: A History of Insanity in the Age of Reason.* Translated by R. Howard, 1988. New York, NY: Vintage Books, 1965.

Frankle, W. G., J. Lerma and M. Laruelle. "The Synaptic Hypothesis of Schizophrenia." *Neuron* 39 (2003): 205–16.

Freud, S. "Beyond the Pleasure Principle." In *Complete Psychological Works*, Vol. 18, 7–64. London: Hogarth Press, 1955 [1920].

Fried, I. et al. "Electrical Current Stimulates Laughter." *Nature* 391 (1998): 650.

Fromm-Reichmann, F. "Notes on the Development of Treatment of Schizophrenics by Psychoanalytic Psychotherapy." *Psychiatry* 11 (1948): 263–73.

Frotscher, M. "Role for Reelin in Stabilizing Cortical Architecture." *Trends in Neurosciences* 33 (2010): 407–14.

Gallo, K. M. "First Person Account: Self-Stigmatization." *Schizophrenia Bulletin* 20 (1994): 407–10.

Gazzaniga, M. S. *The Ethical Brain.* New York, NY: Dana Press, 2005.

Goldston, D. "The Scientist Delusion." *Nature* 452 (2008): 17.

Gottesman, I. I. *Schizophrenia Genesis: The Origins of Madness.* New York, NY: W.H. Freeman & Co., 1991.

Greeley, A. M. and M. Hout. "Americans' Increasing Belief in Life after Death: Religious Competition and Acculturation." *American Sociological Review* 64 (1999): 813–35.

Harrison, P. J. "The Neuropathology of Schizophrenia: A Critical Review of the Data and Their Interpretation." *Brain* 122 (1999): 593–624.

Harrison, P. J. and D. R. Weinberger. "Schizophrenia Genes, Gene Expression, and Neuropathology: On the Matter of Their Convergence." *Molecular Psychiatry* 10 (2005): 40–68.

Hart, W. D. *The Engines of the Soul.* Cambridge, England: Cambridge University Press, 1988.

Heider, F. and M. Simmel. "An Experimental Study of Apparent Behavior." *American Journal of Psychology* 57 (1944): 243–59.

Hinshaw, S. P. *The Mark of Shame: Stigma of Mental Illness and an Agenda for Change.* New York, NY: Oxford University Press, 2007.

Huber, S. "Stigma, Society, and Specialty Choice: What's Going On?" *Virtual Mentor* 5, no. 10 (2003), http://virtualmentor.ama-assn.org/2003/10/medu1-0310.html.

Humphrey, N. *Seeing Red: A Study in Consciousness.* Cambridge, MA: Harvard University Press, 2006.

Hyman, S. E. "A Glimmer of Light for Neuropsychiatric Disorders." *Nature* 455 (2008): 890–3.

Insel, T. R. "Disruptive Insights in Psychiatry: Transforming a Clinical Discipline." *Journal of Clinical Investigation* 119 (2009): 700–5.

———. "Faulty Circuits." *Scientific American* 302 (2010a): 44–51.

———. "Rethinking Schizophrenia." *Nature* 468 (2010b): 187–93.

Jackson, F. "Mental Causation." *Mind* 105 (1996): 377–413.

Jaynes, J. *The Origin of Consciousness in the Breakdown of the Bicameral Mind.* Boston, MA: Houghton Mifflin, 1982.

Jennings, D. "The Confusion between Disease and Illness in Clinical Medicine." *Canadian Medical Association Journal* 135 (1986): 865–70.

Kandel, E. R. "A New Intellectual Framework for Psychiatry." *The American Journal of Psychiatry* 155 (1998): 457–69.

———. "Biology and the Future of Psychoanalysis: A New Intellectual Framework for Psychiatry Revisited." *The American Journal of Psychiatry* 156 (1999): 505–24.

———. "The Molecular Biology of Memory Storage: A Dialogue between Genes and Synapses." *Science* 294 (2001): 1030–8.

Kendell, R. E. "The Distinction between Mental and Physical Illness." *British Journal of Psychiatry* 178 (2001): 490–93.

Kendler, K. S. "Toward a Philosophical Structure for Psychiatry." *The American Journal of Psychiatry* 162 (2005): 433–40.

Kim, J. *Physicalism, or Something Near Enough*. Princeton, NJ: Princeton University Press, 2005.

———. "Mental Causation." In *The Oxford Handbook of Philosophy of Mind*, edited by B. P. McLaughlin, A. Beckermann, and S. Walter, 29–52. New York: Oxford University Press, 2009.

Kim, Y. and G. E. Berrios. "Impact of the Term *Schizophrenia* on the Culture of Ideograph: The Japanese Experience." *Schizophrenia Bulletin* 27 (2001): 181–5.

Klempan, T. A., P. Muglia and J. L. Kennedy. "Genes and Brain Development." In *Neurodevelopment and Schizophrenia*, edited by M. S. Keshavan, J. L. Kennedy, and R. M. Murray, 3–34. Cambridge: Cambridge University Press, 2004.

Koch, C. *The Quest for Consciousness: A Neurobiological Approach*. Englewood, CO: Roberts & Co., 2004.

Kudlien, F. "Krankheitsmetaphorik im Laurentiushymnus des Prudentius." *Hermes* 90 (1962): 104–15.

Leech, G., P. Rayson and A. Wilson. *Word Frequencies in Written and Spoken English*. London: Longman, 2001.

Lewis, D. A. and P. Levitt. "Schizophrenia as a Disorder of Neurodevelopment." *Annual Review of Neuroscience* 25 (2005): 409–32.

Link, B. G. et al. "Public Conceptions of Mental Illness: Labels, Causes, Dangerousness, and Social Distance." *American Journal of Public Health* 89 (1999): 1328–33.

Lisman, J. E. et al. "Circuit-Based Framework for Understanding Neurotransmitter and Risk Gene Interactions in Schizophrenia." *Cell* 31 (2008): 234–42.

Littlewood, R. "Cultural Variation in the Stigmatization of Mental Illness." *The Lancet* 352 (1998): 1056–7.

Logothetis, N. K. "What We Can Do and What We Cannot Do with fMRI." *Nature* 453 (2008): 869–78.

Malaspina, D. et al. "Acute Maternal Stress in Pregnancy and Schizophrenia in Offspring: A Cohort Prospective Study." *BMC Psychiatry* 8 (2008): 71.

Malebranche, N. *The Search After Truth*. Edited and translated by T. M. Lennon and P. J. Olscamp. Cambridge, England: Cambridge University Press, 1997 [1674].

McLaughlin, B. P., A. Beckermann, and S. Walter, *The Oxford Handbook of Philosophy of Mind.* New York, NY: Oxford University Press, 2009.

Miresco, M. J. and L. J. Kirmayer. "The Persistence of Mind-Brain Dualism in Psychiatric Reasoning about Clinical Scenarios." *The American Journal of Psychiatry* 163 (2006): 913–8.

Nature (editorial). "A Decade for Psychiatric Disorders." *Nature* 463 (2010): 9.

Nicosia, G. *Memory Babe: A Critical Biography of Jack Kerouac.* Berkeley, CA: University of California Press, 1994.

Nietzsche, F. *The Gay Science.* Translated by W. Kaufmann. New York, NY: Vintage, 1974 [1887].

Nordt, C., W. Rössler and C. Lauber. "Attitudes of Mental Health Professionals toward People with Schizophrenia and Major Depression." *Schizophrenia Bulletin* 32 (2006): 709–14.

Paus, T., M. Keshavan and J. N. Giedd. "Why Do Many Psychiatric Disorders Emerge During Adolescence?" *Nature Reviews Neuroscience* 9 (2008): 947–57.

Penfield, W. *The Excitable Cortex in Conscious Man.* Liverpool: Liverpool University Press, 1958.

———. *The Mystery of the Mind: A Critical Study of Consciousness and the Human Brain.* Princeton, NJ: Princeton University Press, 1975.

Pescosolido et al. "'A Disease Like Any Other'? A Decade of Change in Public Reactions to Schizophrenia, Depression, and Alcohol Dependence." *American Journal of Psychiatry* 167 (2010): 1321–30.

Petronis, A. "Epigenetics as a Unifying Principle in the Aetiology of Complex Traits and Diseases." *Nature* 465 (2010): 721–7.

Pink, T. *Free Will: A Very Short Introduction.* New York, NY: Oxford University Press, 2004.

Popper, K. R. and J. C. Eccles. *The Self and Its Brain: An Argument for Interactionism.* Berlin: Springer-Verlag, 1977.

Porter, R. *Mind-Forg'd Manacles: A History of Madness in England from the Restoration to the Regency.* London: Athlone, 1987.

Potkin, S. G. and J. M. Ford. "Widespread Cortical Dysfunction in Schizophrenia: The FBIRN Imaging Consortium." *Schizophrenia Bulletin* 35 (2009): 15–8.

Roccatagliata, G. *A History of Ancient Psychiatry.* Westport, CT: Greenwood Press, 1986.

Russell, B. *A History of Western Philosophy.* New York, NY: Simon and Shuster, 1945.

Ryle, G. *The Concept of Mind.* London: Hutchinson, 1949.

Sanes, D. H., T. A. Reh and W. A. Harris. *Development of the Nervous System.* 2nd ed. Burlington, MA: Elsevier Academic Press, 2006.

Schomerus, G., H. Matschinger and M. C. Angermeyer. "Traces of Freud—The Unconscious Conflict as a Cause of Mental Disorders in the Eyes of the General Public. *Psychopathology* 41 (2008): 173–8.

Searle, J. "Consciousness and the Philosophers." *New York Review of Books* 44, no. 4 (1997): 60–1.

Selemon L. D., G. Rajkowska and P. S. Goldman-Rakic. "Elevated Neuronal Density in Prefrontal Area 46 in Brains from Schizophrenic Patients: Application of a Three-Dimensional, Stereologic Counting Method." *Journal of Comparative Neurology* 392 (1998): 402–12.

Shettleworth, S. J. *Cognition, Evolution, and Behavior.* 2nd ed. New York, NY: Oxford University Press, 2010.

Shi, J. et al. "Common Variants on Chromosome 6p22.1 are Associated with Schizophrenia." *Nature* 460 (2009): 753–7.

Shorter, E. *A History of Psychiatry: From the Era of the Asylum to the Age of Prozac.* New York, NY: John Wiley & Sons, 1997.

Shorter, E. and D. Healy. *Shock Therapy: A History of Electroconvulsive Treatment in Mental Illness.* New Brunswick, NJ: Rutgers University Press, 2007.

Shweder, R. A. et al. "The 'Big Three' of Morality (Autonomy, Community, Divinity) and the 'Big Three' Explanations of Suffering." In *Morality and Health,* edited by A. Brandt and P. Rozin, 119–69. New York: Routledge, 1997.

Sigurdsson, T. et al. "Impaired Hippocampal-Prefrontal Synchrony in a Genetic Mouse Model of Schizophrenia." *Nature* 464 (2010): 763–7.

Simon, B. *Mind and Madness in Ancient Greece: The Classical Roots of Modern Psychiatry.* Ithaca, NY: Cornell University Press, 1978.

Skinner, B. F. *Beyond Freedom and Dignity.* New York, NY: Knopf, 1971.

Stefansson, H. et al. "Large Recurrent Microdeletions Associated with Schizophrenia." *Nature* 455 (2008): 232–6.

———. "Common Variants Conferring Risk of Schizophrenia." *Nature* 460 (2009): 744–7.

Sullivan, P. F. et al. "*NCAM1* and Neurocognition in Schizophrenia." *Biological Psychiatry* 61 (2007): 902–10.

Szasz, T. S. *The Myth of Mental Illness: Foundations of a Theory of Personal Conduct.* New York, NY: Hoeber-Harper, 1961.

———. *Schizophrenia: The Sacred Symbol of Psychiatry.* New York, NY: Basic Books, 1976.

Takahashi, H. et al. "Impact of Changing the Japanese Term for 'Schizophrenia' for Reasons of Stereotypical Beliefs of Schizophrenia in Japanese Youth." *Schizophrenia Research* 112 (2009): 149–52.

The International Schizophrenia Consortium. "Common Polygenic Variation Contributes to Risk of Schizophrenia and Bipolar Disease." *Nature* 460 (2009): 748–52.

The Wellcome Trust Case Control Consortium. "Genome-Wide Association Study of CNVs in 16,000 Cases of Eight Common Diseases and 3,000 Shared Controls." *Nature* 464 (2010): 713–20.

Van Gulick, R. "Functionalism." In *The Oxford Handbook of Philosophy of Mind*, edited by B. P. McLaughlin, A. Beckermann, and S. Walter, 128–51. New York, NY: Oxford University Press, 2009.

Walker, E. F. and D. Diforio. "Schizophrenia: A Neural Diathesis-Stress Model." *Psychological Review* 104 (1997): 667–85.

Walsh, T. et al. "Rare Structural Variants Disrupt Multiple Genes in Neurodevelopmental Pathways in Schizophrenia." *Science* 320 (2008): 539–43.

Weiner, B. *Judgments of Responsibility: A Foundation for a Theory of Social Conduct.* New York, NY: Guilford Press, 1995.

Weiner, B., R. P. Perry and J. Magnusson. "An Attributional Analysis of Reactions to Stigmas." *Journal of Personality and Social Psychology* 55 (1988): 738–48.

Wilford, J. N. "Found: An Ancient Monument to the Soul." *The New York Times*, November 18, 2008.

Williams, B. *Descartes: The Project of Pure Enquiry.* Hassocks, England: Harvester Press, 1978.

Yoo, J. "Anomalous Monism." In *The Oxford Handbook of Philosophy of Mind*, edited by B. P. McLaughlin, A. Beckermann, and S. Walter, 95–108. New York, NY: Oxford University Press, 2009.

Zilboorg, G. *A History of Medical Psychology.* New York, NY: W.W. Norton & Co., 1941.

Zimmer, C. *Soul Made Flesh: The Discovery of the Brain and How It Changed the World.* London: Free Press, 2004.

Index